.GRAY, THE

The Bereolaesque Group, LLC

1401 Riverplace Blvd.

Jacksonville, FL 32207

Bereolaesque.com

LIBRARY OF CONGRESS CATALOGING-IN-PUBLICATION DATA
has been applied for.

Enitan O. Bereola II
The Gray: A Relationship Etiquette Study
Edited by: Charlina Allen Pruitt
Published by: The Bereolaesque Group, LLC

ISBN: 0692809171
ISBN-13: 978-0692809174

Printed in the United States of America

Let's talk.

Meet me halfway.

GRAY, THE

A RELATIONSHIP ETIQUETTE STUDY

Inspired by,

Us

Composed by,

Enitan O. Bereola, II

Co-written by,

You

ALSO BY ENITAN O. BEREOLA II:
Award-Winning | Best-Selling Literature

GENTLEWOMAN: Etiquette for a Lady, from a Gentleman

BEREOLAESQUE: The Contemporary Gentleman & Etiquette Book for the Urban Sophisticate

Bereolaesque.com

PRAISE

In lieu of praise for the book, the praise goes to God

Everything is not resolved

GRAY.

| grā |

ADJECTIVE

1. COLORLESS

2. CONFUSING

3. DEATHLY

4. DISORDERLY

5. DOUBTFUL

6. DREARY

7. MONOTONOUS

8. SOMBER

9. UNCLEAR

10. WISE

Torn pages from this book belong in galleries, behind glass, protected by red ropes.

This book is an ode to my father:
"Life is about relationship."

—

Be Careful When Judging a Book by its Cover

Sometimes shit is not black and white.

The finest trick I ever pulled is convincing the world I do not exist. I am everywhere. Though you cannot see me, you will feel me. I am a heavy burden of nothing – the author of confusion and manufacturer of assumptions. It might not be OK! Do not attempt to sleep me away. You cannot weep me away. You cannot think me away. You cannot drink me away. You cannot hope me away. You cannot smoke me away. If you are aloof, you will deny me and I will not depart from you. If you are curious, you will read me. You will discover me. You will acknowledge me. You will find the only way to get through me is to get to me.

Watch your step.

-The gray area

CONFIDENTIALITY NOTICE

You are now entering the gray area. The content of this book is exclusively intended for the entity of whom it is addressed. You were deliberately considered when constructing its invaluable scribing. This subject matter contains privileged material to be used for healing mankind. Any unauthorized use is prohibited beyond this point. If you are not the intended recipient, you are hereby notified to read along anyway. You are held with the responsibility of transforming literature into lifestyle, impacting relationships one gentlewoman and gentleman at a time. For this is not just a product—this is your protection.

—

CONTENTS

JIDENNA

Manifesto: By Jidenna

Where did we go wrong?

Class ain't just a glass of champagne. It is more about taste and discretion.

The Classic Man is a distinguished gentleman. He keeps his gloves dirty, but his hands clean. He is absolutely certain that less is more, that actions speak louder than words and that quality is better than quantity. He avoids making excuses and accepts both praise and criticism with the same cool. A Classic Man is observant, so he is naturally concerned with the details of his appearance and the presentation of his reputation. Thus, he is sharp in mind, body and style.

The Classic Man is the man that steps up to care for that which is not his own. He is the street elegant old-fashioned man, the urban sophisticate. He is a man that every man wants to be and every woman wants to be with. To both his lovers and his enemies, his charm is a necessary evil. Under fire, the Classic Man remains cool as Nat King Cole. He sons immature men without them knowing they've just been sonned. He can pull the wool or be a bull while being polite. A Classic Man never rants in public; he delivers speeches with passion and conviction.

The Classic Man holds women in the highest of regard and will lay down his life to protect them. He believes that great women are the backbone of a successful nation. While others struggle to admit it, he believes that women are generally wiser and more loyal than men. Regardless of sexual orientation, boys and young men struggle with maintaining valuable, platonic relationships with women. Many do not have the male role models or father figures that teach exactly how to relate with the opposite sex, let alone a potential mate. Classic Men are usually found in the company of brilliant, successful women.

While other men cannot control their hormones in the presence of beauty, the Classic Man can stare into your eyes and hold an enlightening conversation without making a pass. He feels no need to hunt on the prowl; his patience and wit capture your heart and mind. He takes his mates on adventures, not dates. He knows that texting is not courting and courtship is not a means to an end. Well, on second thought, it is … but the key to wooing is to focus on the present moment. It is extremely challenging to civilize one's primal desire especially after a few drinks. The more you hold out, however, the more you will be desired and ultimately rewarded. Once you invite him in and ask him to check his coat at the door, he understands that he can finally check some of his manners as well. To quote Enitan Bereola, "Etiquette has no place in the bedroom." It is usually at this point that you realize that the Classic Man is still a man and that Man is still an animal.

-Jidenna,
Classic Man

Grammy nominated / award-winning recording artist, record producer, actor and Master of Ceremony

FOREWORD

Hypothesis | *Elephants are pink in small rooms.*

PRELUDE

PRELUDE // WALLS

He needed a ghostwriter.
So much to say, but it was so chaotic in his head.
She needed a ghostwriter.
Her legs were spread and then nothing was said.
He needed a ghostwriter.
He spoke with passion, but didn't know where the periods went.
She needed a ghostwriter.
She didn't know how to tell him where her period went.
He needed a ghostwriter.
There was little time to tell it all.
She needed a ghostwriter…
Except she didn't want to tell at all.
Do you need a ghostwriter?
A voice of reason to reveal your story?
I'll be your ghostwriter.
I'll take the burden.
You get the glory.

Let's begin…

Have a seat.

Please, get comfortable.

This is an honest, overdue conversation between two strangers – you and me. I promise to be open and I ask that you do the same. No judgment. You will not be shamed. This is your safe space. It is only you and I here.

Allow me to be the first to admit guilt. In an effort to rebuild you, I destroyed us. My first two books proved a few things. They are critically acclaimed and award-winning bestsellers owned by elites from Oprah Winfrey to The Obamas. They were written to dig holes in mental mountains and cause walls of mis-education to crumble. The books became so self-empowering that it made independence trendy. That is cool. The problem is some readers became soaked with self-absorption.

Drenched.

In an age of self-reliance, we find it weak to acknowledge our neediness. The response to my last work proved our desire to love ourselves, but failed to prove the need for us to love each other.

You have since rebuilt more improved and elaborate walls to protect your newfound light resulting in a dark society. For now you are doing fine in your sheltered bubble, but it will burst. Hail will rain on your parade and your glow will fade. Relationships will suffer. I gave you lemonade without teaching you how to squeeze the lemons to make your own jug. I fed you fish, but failed to teach you how to fish. I have been entrusted with impregnating you with a seed of hope to birth a revolution, and like post-pregnancy breasts, I left you hanging –beautiful, but hanging.

So I wrote you the book that I need to read – we need to read.

The Gray is a sobering study of real relationships and where we went wrong.

Humanity is not connecting as a culture, country, community, nor as companions or as couples. There is a general sense of dissatisfaction in the world. People are deeply divided, terrified, disturbed, horrified, disheartened, annoyed and disgusted in these divided states of America and yonder. We are afraid of each other.

This literature aims to pierce through the noise; the clutter; the chaos.

I introduce two characters in this chilling account – masculine and feminine. The story is loosely based on a gentleman who has read my first book and a gentlewoman who has read my second book. Their interaction is thought to maintain the harmony of the universe and influence everything within it as yin and yang suggests. But dogma can be challenged in the gray area.

The world is at war for your attention. Television, radio and the Internet fight for access daily. They pay top dollar for only a moment of your time. Even in solitude you are susceptible to your own thoughts.

When your space gets gray, drop what you are doing and pick this up.

This book is written to protect your magic and center your spirit without compromising your light. Unplug everything and turn off your Wi-Fi. Get quiet and listen. When your mind wanders, bring it back by focusing on deep breathing until you feel a loud whisper. It will be an affirming voice, not negative noise. The voice will answer tough questions and provide clarity on important decisions. It might be one word. It could be a quiet soliloquy. The more you take time to listen, the clearer the voice will become.

My writing style is black and white – right and wrong. Wrong is the act of not getting it right. But not getting it right is not always wrong – plain and simple. To put it simply plain, not everything is black and white. *The Gray* is somewhere between truth and fiction. It is an unsolved mystery complete with that eerie theme song hosted by Robert Stack.

Until now.

INTRODUCTION

Introduction // Theory

*– "I'm sure there's some self-help cheese-ball book about the gray area." –*Justin Timberlake

This is not that.

The story you are about to experience is inspired by true events; only the names have been changed to protect the innocent. It is a saga of betrayal and redemption. It is set in the past, present and future. It is history. It is his story. It is her story. It is your story. It is my story. This story is all of our stories. I sat with thousands of couples – some famous, others everyday people. Data was collected and the theories in each chapter have been tested. If the plot troubles you, it is supposed to. If you become uncomfortable while reading, you are meant to. If this story alters all you believe to be true, so be it. When literature literally heals you, please understand it is crafted to. Let the ink from each word and every sentence drip off the pages to saturate a soul and create a new song. What happens from here is predestined. You did not come this far only to come this far. The reason I wrote this is the reason you are reading it. Everything in your life up to this instant has led to now. This book. This moment.

"Write away right away."

"It is urgent this time, but this will take time."

These were my thoughts while on a three-year hiatus from manuscripts, gallivanting the globe and discussing etiquette. Now we are in the age of self-help. Bookstores flood with paperbacks about taking care of number one, curing unhappiness by making oneself the center of all things. The idea is to create a more confident culture, but the cure came with side effects. Even I got high off my own supply. No disrespect to Notorious B.I.G.

My mission for civilization to be self-sufficient, not self-serving got drowned out by standing ovations and Retweets. We are increasingly becoming a more selfish society impaired by empowerment. Independence overdose is at an all time high and our tolerance is lower than the hairline of a Neanderthal. It is nothing to cut a line off. Squares decreased their circle as soon as a hit song said, "No new friends." No help. No, thank you. We are a throw-away culture that discards things that can be repaired – like shoes and humans. We suppress the desire to connect as a survival mechanism. Doing life alone has become a reality we pretend to accept. It was never my intention for egocentricity to become a theme in my message.

I apologize.

I braced you for the plunge, but I did not prepare you for the impact.

Forgive me.

I pushed you to fall perpetually in love with yourself again, again and again, and all over again with a dash of a pen. One by one, I watched as you soared. I encouraged you on your journey as you prepared to present the world your authentic self with some manners. I lent you inspiration and sold you similes. We met at 4:00 with metaphors as you read more until your crown was straightened. You allowed me to tour your thoughts and take my conclusions on tour in small states and big countries. I lectured in London and powwowed in private places. For two presidential terms, we communicated and created solutions. I listened. I learned. I watched. We dug deep. And this is what I know for sure:

We need love.

No, not a simple regard for our own well-being and happiness, but an itch to accept and return love like a parent to child. You are seeking a connection more secure than airport terminal Wi-Fi. You are over "Hey stranger" text messages and quick contact – that is cool for a callow kid, except you are a full-blown adult. Your soul yearns for a love with a slow burn like grandma's Sunday cooking. You need a satisfaction that lasts after the encounter like grandma's Sunday cooking. You need a feeling that puts you to sleep, then wakes you up after four seconds for seconds like grandma's Sunday cooking. A warm, comforting allegiance is all you have time for.

I WRITE FOR THE PEOPLE

To walk in your shoes I had to borrow your souls. I know how desolate it can be. You showed me. I could feel it in each stride as I ran from the issues. Like a method actor becomes his or her character, a writer becomes his or her audience. It is like entering the mind of an adulterer, abused child or rape victim – or attempting to channel the spirit of a racist or bully. The process is uncomfortable, but it increases perspective and empathy. The goal is to balance the scales of equality. I believe in fairness. I trust that negative questions

29

have positive solutions so I write about them. Light casts out darkness so I shine.

This conversation piece is a piece of art studying the art of relationships and what causes us to connect to, or disconnect from one another. This is not the typical "I love you; you love me" storybook. This certainly is not your average "how to" guide. This literature sets out to awaken your conscience, inspire intimacy and challenge the way society treats itself. This story was produced to improve relationships whether professional, platonic or passionate. The reality is that we are in this thing called life together. Our existence is intertwined. We impact each other in ways beyond hellos, sexual encounters and pleasantries. Our association is not all about business and banter, or cordially asking how a stranger is doing when we care less about the response. You are my oxygen. Though I may never see you, I need you in order to breathe. I am your water. My tasteless delivery is transparent. In order to survive you need me. Life comes down to this statement. In order to eat, we need each other.

Most are denied a seat at the table. Society seems more interested in breaking bones than breaking bread.

COMMUNICATION IS HOW WE CONNECT

Like Black lives, we pretend words do not matter. We hurl them out as if they do not stick; as if they do not burn; as if we do not bleed. The world has become one large comment section filled with criticism. How do we connect if we cannot talk?

I blame the Internet.

Communication is our most powerful tool and yet we still do not know how it works. We have a head, body, mouth, tongue, lips and eyes, but will not make personal contact at a dinner table due to a needless need to connect to a wireless device and view the latest post from the person sitting next to us so we can repost it and the rest of the table can discuss us in the comments. ☺

Every day, my good faith in people is snatched from me because too often I am reminded of how obtuse we are. How is it that we are so connected to the technology that connects us closer to the world, yet we are more disconnected than ever? People remember to log into social media, then forget to be social in real life. We suffocate our citizens by silencing them with cell phones. Ironic. I will be the first to admit guilt. Sometimes I am too committed to my handheld to get my hand held.

More often than not, I am fumbling to put my phone in my pocket to free my hand when meeting someone for the first time. To seek common ground, I fish for familiarity until finding something I can relate to. I search for a shared interest in sports by asking if a stranger saw the game last. I ask where someone is from to determine if I have a connection to his or her hometown. A relationship is a quest to discover us through others. Essentially, we use relationships as a mirror to help see who we are and ultimately improve our environment. Subconsciously, this demonstration is the reason we connect.

YOU ARE THE COMPANY YOU KEEP

Some of my closest friends from grammar school are now strangers viewed on Facebook. My real friends are companions for reasons other than growing up in the same neighborhood.

Everything in life is connected and we find ourselves through identifying with others. Socializing with smart people either reinforces our intellect or allows us to learn. If we are rebellious, we fraternize with rebels to reinforce our beliefs about our worldview and ourselves. Politically, we associate with the party that best resembles who we are or strive to be. If we are curious, we connect to everything, including opposing views that challenge our perspective.

But hurt people reinforce separation.

Rejection is not a simple refusal to accept someone or something. Instead, it is an internalized belief that a person or group's life does not matter and the decision has been made to deny all that they are and ever hope to be.

This generation is filled with hardened hate groups, tacky Internet trolls and bullies who appear to care about nothing and no one. Oh, but they do. Picking fights is often a demonstration of one's inability to say, "Let's be friends." They despise the idea of a disconnection so much that they are willing to confront and destroy anything that is detached from them.

Some of my greatest friends began as enemies.

Showing respect and loyalty is the most masculine way to tell another man, "I love you." "I need you." "I want to stay connected with you forever." We communicate in code, but there is no substitute for trust. A man will kill over betrayal. It is a false connection. That is why we pride ourselves on keeping it real.

So if you claim not to care what anyone thinks of you, then you are likely running from reality on rocks with no shoes on.

It hurts.

Admit it.

Relationships matter.

We all care whether the people we care about care about us. We pretend we do not as a defense mechanism to deal with rejection. But that proves we care. Nonchalance is a coping system. So is indifference. You convince yourself you do not care to avoid the inconvenience of caring about someone who does not care about you. If you saw yourself as people see you, you might see things differently. But you avoid that pain by denying it exists. Now you are a three-time liar – you are dishonest with yourself, others and the person you pretend to hate. That is how deeply innate our need for connection is.

The rise in popularity of social networking displays our desire to connect to something – preferably people. People like people they can identify with. We have a propensity to be fond of others, but others do not always make themselves easy to be fond of.

Ask yourself why you are unable to connect with someone. Do you have a valid reason other than you just do not like the person? Is it because they do not like you, and like a second-grader, you decide not to like them back? The only real way to show you do not care what someone thinks of you is by loving them anyway. Love disarms. When you respond to hate with hate, you are giving up your power to love. If you truly have no interest in someone's opinion about you, then their opinion would not affect yours.

I have never met a happy hater or a cute critic. All of these blogs. All of these opinions. All of these strangers. If you have ever seen a critic, you would understand why they are so critical. They marinate their lives in misery and grow upset with you for being dope and free. They become irritated as you celebrate your authenticity and unapologetically be yourself. You confuse them, so they study you. Here is what they should know:

A good connection seeks to put forth and receive back a positive response. A bad connection puts out and receives back a negative response. This is a universal truth regardless of one's beliefs. Some people call it cause and effect – some call it karma – some call it reaping and sowing. The cognoscenti call it *The Golden Rule*. Whatever you call it, it is the philosophy that allows you to believe in something greater than yourself. Only grace returns a positive response after receiving a negative one.

Connections establish the boundaries of right and wrong that dictate our belief system. We call them morals and values. When our son took his first steps, my wife and I filled with unspeakable joy. We roared a loud applause and his face lit up with love. Due to the favorable experience, our son continues to look to us for positive reinforcement when he walks. But when our son puts a foreign object in his mouth and we yell, "No!" in an aggressive tone, he acknowledges the disconnection and responds with his bottom lip poked out. We are teaching him right versus wrong as he finds his place in our lives and this world. This is basic relationship etiquette.

Here is where it gets tricky. If our son believes he is doing something good (like standing up in his high chair) and we respond negatively, it creates confusion with our connection, causing him to pull back and detach. That is the problem with good intention. It does not mean the harm it causes. When we fail to clearly communicate our actions, we enter a gray area.

Humanity exists within the gray. People are complicated. It is not always either or, right or wrong, good or bad. Kill the binary narrative. This is not mathematics. This is biology and chemistry. We are living organisms and that is some messy shit.

Please excuse my French.

There is an art to communication. It is a dance that requires the techniques of rhythm, prediction and improvisation. You must know when to step in and take the lead, or pull back and shut up.

Shutting up is a lost art.

It is simple to learn.

I can teach you.

ETIQUETTE GOVERNS RELATIONSHIPS

It is the protocol for establishing, managing and maintaining a connection.

We all know people who are great at initiating relationships, but have no skill in preserving them. They take your number and never use it. Or those who seize relationships for dominance and control. They possess no interest in actual leadership. These people collect colleagues, but offer no service, support or sustenance like a certain cable company.

Never more than ever is this literature more necessary than now.

So we begin again.

We start anew.

I present you the book that did not want to be written.

END OF AUGUST

END OF AUGUST //
ALTERNATE THURSDAY

T he roads were quiet. Wind nestled through dry leaves as peculiar clouds broke through September's sky. A faded sun poured champagne across the distance coloring the heavens. Summer, they said. It'll be warm, they said. It was brisk when a boy met a girl.

"What are you doing here?" His inelegant introduction went ignored.

A svelte little lady slammed the passenger door in the driveway across from his. Her hair was black. A frail, gray-haired woman who looked to be in her mid-fifties got out of the driver's side carrying two books. She was more handsome than pretty. The back seat was filled to the roof with junk.

"Are you gonna stand there or help us carry all this shit?" The handsome older woman yelled to the boy.

There was baggage – lots of baggage. And the shit looked heavy!

"Let me get my father to help." The boy ran inside his home, dropping wet rags from washing his car. He returned with a man with a mustache that scolded him for running water after six o'clock. They were experiencing a drought in their state. It hadn't rained all summer.

But a storm was coming.

"You need help with your shit?" The boy's father stood with narrow eyes despite a lack of sunshine. He didn't appear capable of lifting a thing. Sometimes being a gentleman is inconvenient.

"I do."

It was the beginning of the end of summer when the new neighbors moved in. The girl was always quiet and angry and the mother was always quite angry. The boy usually overheard them arguing about the girl's father when he'd drop her off outside her big red front door. Her parents used her as a chess piece in their divorce. It was less about love and more about leverage. She grew familiar being pulled in opposite directions. Imbalance became a steady place for her.

And it showed.

She was the new girl at school. Everyone knew, and everyone knew that everyone knew. He was a senior and she was a freshman. Fresh men ten years her senior gawked when she galloped on by. She wore an innocent smirk, but traveled with a sinister stride in pink trousers. The older male counselors and graying cafeteria guys tried so hard not to look so hard. She had a body like reality TV – you didn't want to watch, but you had to. When men both young and old saw her, they knew. She knew they knew she had dumb ass like a donkey, but she was no dumb ass. She was the type to mind her business, do yoga, fuck shit up and drink green juice. She wasn't concerned with the typical gossip guys do. She didn't care for "locker room talk." She was interested in real conversation with real people – the type of dining table discussions that leave you full before the meal comes. She seemed like she knew who she was, so he couldn't dare approach her like he didn't. He studied her body language and matched her rhythm until finding the perfect moment to use the best pickup line in the book to address the fat pink elephant in the room.

"Hello."

Her eyes moved toward his, but her head remained still.

He grew anxious in two places.

"Sooo did you catch the basketball game last night?"

That's all he had.

It was the dawn of football season. Basketball didn't start for almost two months. The girl giggled and the elephant in the room lost weight.

The boy and his neighbor shared a smile.

WHEN A MOUTH TURNS THE CORNER, A RELATIONSHIP TURNS THE CORNER

He started walking home at the same time the girl walked home. They were headed in the same direction anyway. Except he played hooky during last period to ensure he was there when she took her first step.

Initial exchanges were innocuous. He engaged her with simple chitchat about shortcuts through the neighborhood. But the shortcuts got cut short when their conversations became long. After a while, they began taking the long way home until home felt like a long way home. She explained why she hated her mother for leaving her father. They moved to town so her mom could receive decent cancer treatment. He told her he was rethinking college the following year. He was managing and producing a local band. Plus his dad was getting older and needed him around the house.

"They should get married." She laughed. "My mom and your dad."

"Nah, I'm not trying to be your brother."

His eyes smiled before his mouth did.

It was like one of those talks you have in parked cars with your best friend. Time was but a suggestion. Mouths couldn't keep up with thoughts and ideas flowed freely when they felt this freedom – freedom from judgment; liberation from guilt; and deliverance from adults. It was a necessary departure, still they didn't have to go far – only closer to each other.

They got lost in the right direction.

When she found him, she didn't tell anyone about him.

No announcements.

No photos.

Just them.

What they shared was no one's business. It was too personal; too perfect for the world. They bumped into each other in an unlikely place and held on for dear life.

Those who mattered knew. She wasn't exposing him and he wasn't concealing her. Their discretion wasn't intended to hide their connection, but to be wise about the information they shared and with whom they shared it.

Their energy wasn't bound by boundaries. He wasn't just a young man – he was a prototype that commanded observation. And she wasn't just a girl – she was a feeling. Her existence made you combust. Even when silent, her nothing was heavy. And all of that was too delicate to post online for approval.

They put their phones away.

Luring language led them on a path to an even longer way home through a thoroughfare where cellular phones couldn't contaminate their conversation – just a pair of kids connecting offline. They ended up at a bookstore, but didn't buy a thing. On a whim, they whisked away to the local museum to visually consume the art they'd just studied at the bookshop. The boy reached in his book bag and pulled out a black camera. She smiled a hundred times. They laughed like children while enjoying adult conversation, licorice and cheap wine for the first time. Taking the longest way home for the first time. Going on their first date for the third time. They didn't have to go

Dutch. He did more with less by being creative and they had a damn good time before a long walk home.

On the road, their talks turned into something tangible. She vibrated higher and he met at her frequency. Her words were like dives into pools of conversation. He could spill to her about anything, and the more they talked, the more anything could happen. He made her open to anything – including herself. The further they went, the more gorgeous the view. They got deep – where there was no air. No longer could they settle for beautiful babble. Her eyes begged him to connect with more than queries and comments. She longed to inhale his sentences. He needed to attach the instrument she spoke from to the instrument he spoke with. If her lips caged the tongue that created her words, he needed full access.

"Can I show you something?"

She possessed nothing of value so it was easy to be possessed by him. Her trusting hand grabbed his as he ushered her away from familiarity. They traveled a scenic path with oak trees abound. She'd never seen that side of town. An abandoned home came into view as they continued on.

Her memory faded. Her femininity faded.

Thursday's sky choked the sun as daylight surrendered to night's unknown.

What if you had a secret so bad, you forgot it happened?

Her mysteries were hidden in a dark place she learned to forget. Her body held memories that her mind didn't. Archaic ravishment left behind scars she couldn't see so they were easy to ignore.

Her boy friend raped her.

It wasn't so cut and dry, although it cut her dry. She didn't say no and she didn't say yes, but that means no. Yes? He didn't know. Neither did she. It was her first time. He took what she didn't know before she knew it. Before she knew it, he was forcing his torment inside of her tenderness, tearing innocence and rubbing his pain against her wounds. Simplicity bled down immature legs. Purity poured from inside of her. She felt herself shrink. Lifeless eyes stared at the boy who said, "I like you," for the first time only an hour before. Back and forth he mechanically entered and deposited himself like trash. Her head banged violently against a headboard she didn't know. What was happening? The girl no longer recognized what was on top of her. His kiss was cold. His breath was burning. He felt like winter, but tasted like summer. She was absorbed in silence while sheets absorbed her tears mixed with the sweat of his brow. Her core shifted. There was an earthquake in her body. And then it stopped. Her whole frame dimmed as she held her breath. Suddenly everything went black.

A gentleman is just a patient wolf.

"Baby?"

He came while she came to. She awoke without saying a word.

"You OK?" Concern consumed him. His older sister used to touch him when they were younger. She put perversion in him before he could piss in a toilet.

"I'm fine!"

She tucked her head in his chest like a child and he lifted up her chin with careful fingers. He was beautiful, but deathly – like a cashmere noose. They kissed as she artlessly removed crusted panties caked with blood and stains of whatever else was inside of him. His lips were full, but his kisses were empty.

The roads were quiet.

Wind nestled through dry leaves as peculiar clouds broke through September's sky. A waning crescent moon barely lit the heavens.

Summer, they said. It'll be warm, they said.

The mood matched the weather. She knew her mother would be worried so they started back home. This journey was far more silent than the last. Their energy was off and footsteps were out of sync. The rhythm of the night belonged to chirping tree crickets. It was an unusual song she learned to hate.

Streetlights lit a familiar path as a few patio lights appeared in the distance. They were almost home, but felt further than ever. The girl's mother was standing in the driveway in a robe and slippers with a slim cigarette hanging from plum lips. She was gangster like that. Her father was waiting in a pickup truck across the street. He normally arrived Friday nights, but recently arranged to pick her up Thursdays after school. He was a no-show. The mother must've called him out of his sleep to get her. She spoke no words to the girl. She pushed a large suitcase down the driveway, turned off the front lights and shut the red front door.

"Get in."

It was the boy's first and last time seeing the girl's father. Salt and pepper stubble aligned the old man's face. He looked like he had a permanent whiskey smell. The boy wondered how such a pretty girl could come from such ugly parents.

The child of divorce never looked up while she limped her way to her father's truck. It was as if she replayed memories of what happened only moments ago.

Brief encounters form lasting scars.

The truck pulled off in a puff of smoke and the boy watched his future fade into the early morning.

"Wait!"

The boy ran after something that was already gone.
"You forgot something!"

There was a book in the middle of the street, but it was too late. He reached down to grab the cover and noticed its was torn. It was the same book he helped the girl's mother carry when they first moved into town. He brought it in his house, walked by the family photos to his room and threw it at his bedside table.

The boy didn't see the girl at school that Friday. When the bell rang, he walked home with friends pretending to enjoy an afternoon stroll.

But the roads were quiet.

Wind nestled through dry leaves as peculiar clouds broke through the sky.

Summer, they said. It'll be warm, they said.

He never saw the girl again – at least not in the same way.

SPECIFICATION

"There was baggage – lots of baggage. And all the shit looked heavy!"

In the beginning, the girl leaves the boy with her baggage to carry. Her sudden arrival in the driveway across from his represents all the beautiful things that unexpectedly show up in our lives. Unfortunately, beauty often comes with a burden. Life presents something equally unpleasant to distract us from glory.

When the boy helps the girl carry her baggage, I don't want you to focus on the literal baggage, but the figurative weight she's burdened with – both body and mind. She's young with developed breasts and a trunk full of trouble. She's a suffering soul caught in the middle of something. She despises her mother and misses her daddy. Her parents are recently divorced. She prefers attention from men because she has a stronger connection with them. At the end of the chapter, the boy leaves the girl with his baggage to carry.

A relationship is an exchange of energy we call reciprocity. We must pay attention to the energy we receive. It could be a sign of the energy we're giving off. Often, we're unaware we wear the pain we attempt to hide. We subconsciously seek assistance to carry our baggage. Help could be in the form of a friend, family member or lover. And when we find relief, we unload.

Sometimes relief is the motive that stimulates someone to have a relationship in the first place. They're in it to unpack their burdens and leave. There are also those whose motive is to relieve others by taking on their burdens. One motive is selfish and the other is selfless. Know which you're getting and which you're being in order to avoid the gray area. Be discerning by focusing less attention on intention and more on motive. Intention can be deceiving.

"She explained why she hated her mother for leaving her father."

And her mother wasn't president of her daughter's fan club either. Her disdain is subtly stained on pages throughout the chapter. A mother and daughter's relationship is a complex one.

Some mothers desire to be their daughter. Some mothers never wanted a daughter. Some mothers are just like their daughter. Everything they ran away from shows up in the form of a child as a permanent proof of bad decisions. Some mothers compete with their daughter. Some mothers sleep with their daughter. Not in the way a mother is supposed to, but to find out why her father's the only one the daughter's close to.

Some mother.

Some mothers can't stand their daughter. They don't understand their daughter. They can't figure out what went wrong or why they have a man for a daughter.

It's assumed daughters automatically enter into a special bond with their mothers before birth. When a pregnant woman discovers she's having a girl, she dreams of doing hair, hosting sleepovers and picking out wedding dresses.

Not really. This isn't the reality.

Some moms wanted a son. In some cultures, the son is spoiled and the daughter is raised. Some mothers have other reasons. And some don't understand the reason at all.

Mothers are human, too.

Since the time of creation, people have been people and people continue to be people. We must come to the understanding that our parents are people too. They had a life outside of parenting before us, and during the time they raised us. Much of their worldview during the time of conception plays a role in how we were raised.

Viewing our parents as regular folk is unsettling. It's like seeing your fourth-grade teacher at the grocery store, or your doctor at the bar realizing that there's much more to them than the role they play in your life. They're human beings, too.

Just like popes and celebrities.

It's hard to understand the decisions of a parent until you become one. We often think what we'd do differently if we were in their shoes in regards to choices they made raising us. But you can't do that because, well, you're not your parent. You're you. And the best you can do is improve upon the design of your parents by being the best version of yourself.

Pain is passed down through generations until you forgive.

We are able to pardon our parents when we make a concerted effort to empathize with them. Consider what they were going through when you came. Be careful not to compare yourself and what you would've done differently. That ruins the point of putting yourself in their shoes that are suddenly beginning to fit you. Look at who they were back then, where they were in their life and any struggles they could've been dealing with.

If you keep looking, you might see yourself.

"When a mouth turns the corner, a relationship turns the corner."

We all remember a time when we let our guard down for someone we thought was genuine and got our feelings smashed. For some of us, the trauma was too much to bear and we never let anyone get close again. Others are optimistic and remain open to life's beautiful possibilities.

The moment the boy got the girl to smile was the point of no return. A grin appears innocent, but you can never be so sure.
I can relate. I was crazy about women in college. Insane. My philosophy was this: the more, the merrier and life was merry. I wasn't trying to marry. I just wanted a legitimate opportunity to provide the ladies in my life a decent time. Not solely for sexual escapades to hang from ceiling fans, but I enjoyed all the mysteries of feminine energy. If you put the dopest woman in a room with the dopest man, the dope woman will always be doper. It's simple math. A great woman is greater than, or equal to a great man. She doesn't only endure more, but she's just wired differently. Women get it! In my opinion, they're smarter than men. They're also these regal,

ridiculously beautiful flower unicorns from another species that can turn water to wine and winter to summer with a wave.

Hello!

I needed to be around that at all times. Consequently I became accustomed to the high of crumbling walls and conquering kitties. I was a carefree cat. Naturally it increased sexual encounters with pairs of women. Trios. Quartets. Many of them weren't the type to be impressed by a swanky fellow with well-put words. Pardon me, but I wasn't the usual man. I didn't use arrogance as my weapon of choice. I used humility. I served to make women comfortable. It was the only objective. Although the only couch and television at my college home was strategically located in my bedroom, I always offered to sleep on that sofa. And once she was comfortably tucked in my bed, she was consensually mine.

It started with a smile.

And ended with one.

"Luring language led them on a path to an even longer way home through a thoroughfare where cellular phones couldn't contaminate their conversation – just a pair of kids connecting offline. They ended up at a bookstore, but didn't buy a thing. On a whim, they whisked away to the local museum to visually consume the art they'd just studied at the bookshop. The boy reached in his book bag and pulled out a black camera. She smiled a hundred times. They laughed like children while

enjoying adult conversation, licorice and cheap wine for the first time."

SPEND MORE ON EXPERIENCES THAN THINGS.

Bypass the bourgeoisie for a bit. People just want to feel something real! Nothing makes us feel anything anymore. Nothing is authentic. Telling her to pack a small bag is better than buying her a big one. You'll forget about that purse and those shoes. You'll misplace earrings and lose phones, but you'll never lose the memory of a shared experience. You don't forget trips. You don't forget how warm an ocean felt, or how many times you smiled. You remember the relieving sensation of bare feet on new land. You remember the excitement of a plane ride or the taste of a new culture. Those memories stick.

Treat your family to dinner. Spend time with people you love before you spend your paycheck on things. Experience something different. Experience life. Experience God.

"He could spill to her about anything, and the more they talked, the more anything could happen. He made her open to anything – including herself. The further they went, the more gorgeous the view. They got deep – where there was no air."

Be careful going with the flow – the current might steal you.

An ocean's allure can lure you in and suddenly swallow you whole. The clashing of waves is dangerously beautiful. Observe from a safe place, but don't get in. She got in. When we fail to set a standard and enforce who has access to our life, we tend to go with any rhythm that feels good. If there's chemistry, we allow a stranger to study our biology.

GOOD VIBES AND DOPE ENERGY WILL FOOL YOU

Be careful with carefree people. Casual words can spill from their lips to dampen your morals and get you to reconsider your values if only for a moment. The next morning when you're trying to piece yourself together after letting your guard down, they're nowhere to be found – returned to the shadows as quickly as they came. Sometimes a free spirit is just a tortured soul looking for its next victim.

People with no inhibitions love phrases like, "Loosen up," "Don't worry," and "It's all good." So pay attention to what you give attention to by discerning between moments you're slipping further from your center or simply trying something new.

Avoid waves that clash with your own – even when it's beautiful.

A Sunday school teacher once told me to never smoke crack. He also told me the high from smoking crack is the best feeling he's ever felt in his life. Everything that makes you feel good isn't good for you. Good is subjective. To some people with miserable lives, anything that's not bad is good. We often mistake escapism for good energy. A bad person with bad intentions is willing to be good company until you let them in. That's when they devour you. Some people don't even know what good is. They only see what they recognize. I've heard women with perpetual black eyes and bruised lips say, "Although he beats me, I've got a good man."

Beneath it all, he was looking for an excuse. He blamed his flaws on being a Gemini. For him, it removed personal accountability from his life. He accepted his shortcomings without trying to correct them. Instead he passed them onto any sucker willing to listen; connect. And there she was – the perfect host to rid himself of what he hated most.

She made him feel. He never felt before. In return he shoved his karma into her rectum. He made her feel pain, doubt, lust and insecurity. It's all he ever knew, so it's all he knew to give. And she gave it all back when their souls tied.

Evil is persistent. Immorality is presented in all types of ways. If it doesn't get you one way, it'll try another. And another. It comes packaged as friendship, opportunity, graciousness and good sex. Sometimes it looks like family.

This isn't to suggest you should walk around worrying of whatevers, but you shouldn't relax your standards for fleeting moments you'll end up regretting either.

SEPTEMBER

September // Rain

The girl was gone for 742 sunsets. That's two years. It's 24 months. It had been 106 weeks or 17,808 hours. That's over a million minutes and five books full of seconds right up to the moment you read the very next word.

Then a curious car pulled up to the house across the street from his.

A young woman got out of the driver's side door as a flood of strangers poured into her driveway like paparazzi. Her hair was black. The men had on dark suits and the women were mostly draped in coal-colored coats. He never saw their faces. Some cars from the community dropped by to drop off food and flowers.

He watched curiously from his kitchen window. It baffled him to believe his actions in that abandoned house could be the reason all those people showed up. Were they there to comfort his neighbor for what he'd done to her years ago? It didn't make sense. Some people create their own storms then get confused when it rains. That doesn't make sense either. He had no intention of bringing death to innocence and killing feelings during their last encounter. There was a mix of emotions – angst about the reason for her return, and excitement for her comeback.

She was the color of whiskey in the sun. Her beauty was a special set of circumstances. Not the satisfaction derived from a lick of your favorite ice cream, but the glory of looking into a child's eyes after birth. The girl he once knew developed into a young woman and she had a figure worth figuring out. Her new design deserved examination. Courteous winds wrapped a maple red sundress around her frame. Generous daylight lit the fabric enough to reveal what was underneath. She wore a thong tucked in between legs that leaned causing one cheek to hang as a piece of art. Her hair was long like time. His hypothesis stated that it took four minutes to fall when her hands ran through the strands. The conclusion was a controlled spill. He observed gleefully until realizing there was little time to smile in those menacing minutes. The young man was still concerned of his fate.

Old folks say worry causes cancer. They hardly blame it on cigarettes.

This was the time of day the girl's mother would sashay outside in a robe for a midday drag. The young man had brief, but memorable encounters with her whenever he'd take out the trash and fetch the mail. They shared an odd connection. She was an interesting character who only spoke highly of her daughter when she wasn't around. It was as if she loved the girl in her own type of way from a distance. The young man thought about it, but didn't think about it too much. The rare times he saw them together, they hardly dialogued without discord. No doubt the divorce caused a rift in their relationship. Every child needs a little extra love and she probably felt abandoned during the division. She was part of the divorce too. Her mother was too consumed to notice. Instead she became harder on the girl. She tried to make it another learning lesson for her instead of just loving her. Parents don't always improve on the mistakes of their parents. Some don't try at all, and others try too hard and miss. Some get it right in most areas, but neglect other areas. There are millions of adults walking around with childhood scars whether branded intentionally or not. The best any parent can do is give it their all. Unfortunately, sometimes a mother's all isn't enough.

The more the young man thought about it, the more the arguments made sense. She was a tough old lady. Life made her that way. And that's the same way she loved her daughter.

She was a warrior and as it turned out, a worrier. The frail woman didn't have to worry anymore. After a while the boy realized his strange old acquaintance wasn't coming outside. He swayed back and forth whenever he was in deep thought. It soothed him into thinking clearly. As it turned out, those people gathered in the driveway across the street were there to pay respects. The cancer developed into stage IV and the frail gray-haired woman who wouldn't take no for an answer withered away until she was with them no more.

It was her repast.

The sudden realization jolted him from his kitchen window, across the street and through a sea of strangers to her big red front door.

He banged violently as if an opened door would bring the old lady back. There was no answer. Panic and reality set it. Desperate for air, he raised his arm to knock again when a hand grabbed his from behind.

The young man turned with accidental tears coming down his face. He hadn't wept since his mother's death four cruel summers ago.

"You OK?"

Her voice was calming balm for his troubled spirit. There his neighbor stood with a blank face awaiting his response.

"Hi."

It was déjà vu. They met a second time for the first time. This time was different from the last. It was like they were starting all over again.

"I'm sorry about your mother! I just spoke to her a few days ago and we were talking in your driveway, and she was going on and on about how proud of you she was, and…"

"Are you OK?" She cut him off.

He looked into eyes void of emotion desperately trying to find something there. Anything. In a weird way, her mom was like a mother figure to him and he needed someone to mourn with. He searched for a connection in his neighbor, but she was cold as October.

She interrupted the staring contest. "Thanks for coming by. We're going to the cemetery shortly. Why don't I drop by your place later tonight and we'll catch up?"

It was the kind of question that came with an answer.

"Yea, that's cool. I'm not going anywhere."

She was more assertive than he remembered. It was inappropriately sexy. He reached out to embrace her, but she'd already turned around to entertain another guest.

"Do you need us to keep you company later on? We can stay the night to make sure you're alright."

The guest offered a kind gesture. The young man overheard their conversation as he still stood stupidly.

"No, I think I need to be alone."

He felt alone as he turned to walk back home. He got to the garage when he turned to look back once more.

"You gonna stand there or help me carry all this shit?" He yelled from his driveway.

The two of them grinned, remembering a day when the roads were quiet and wind nestled through dry leaves as peculiar clouds broke through the sky.

Eventually, the sun fell. So did expectations of his neighbor dropping by.

"Maybe she fell asleep. She couldn't have forgotten. She couldn't have changed her mind, right?"

He started to sway, but didn't have the answers.

Thoughts went everywhere.

He knew she was home alone.

He grabbed his key, snatched a coat and headed across the street. It was soaking wet outside. The screen door squeaked and the dumb dogs barked a few houses down. The motion detector on an automatic light came on. The rain was heavier than it looked. He started to go back inside for an umbrella, but didn't want to wake up his father.

The girl across the street was still awake. There was more on her mind than most can handle. Her neighbor wasn't one of them. She studied motivational literature while she was away and kept her favorite copy close.

In one moment, the ring of his unexpected doorbell crumbled her walls, turning back pages of self-improvement books. She looked through the peephole and saw her departure from normalcy on the other side. If God were real, he wouldn't allow her to do what she was about to do. She was empty. She was dry. And this man was her humidity. His head was worth the headache. With a defiant mind and an able body, she opened the big red door. There he stood. In he came. And she was back in prison.

She removed his jacket and nothing was underneath. Not a word was spoken.

A tongue and a middle finger were placed in her mouth until discovering a more suitable place to stick them.

She let him fuck deep inside because deep inside she didn't give a fuck. There was nothing there. No feelings. No borders. No boundaries. Two souls sucking each other's face, desperate for air; for life; for something. Anything but yesterday.

She allowed her standards to sink just to ensure the spot next to her in bed did. At fourteen years old, she convinced herself she didn't care about herself. Her submissive outlook was the result of a fatalistic attitude.

It had been a while.

Their bodies were stubborn like the Meeting of Waters. He was the Rio Negro and she was the Rio Solimões. They collided without connecting. She gave him all she had and he gave her all he knew. Sadly, neither of them got the same thing in return.

"You don't have to be cool." She said. "It's warm in there."

He moved with no respect for rhythm. Their second time was worse than the first. It was dry in her bed, but raining outside her window. Why couldn't she trade places with the rain? Why couldn't it be wet in her bed, but stale outside? Her imagination ran wild as he wildly ran inside her. She wanted to feel, but refused to be touched. She couldn't connect, so she closed her eyes and imagined being in a safe place – a place that provided reciprocity. A subtle moan slipped when she finally felt something. Each stroke was a reunion. She could feel how much he missed her. Gradually, then suddenly – he pushed into her walls and she shattered. He opened her. He located all her closures and reopened them. She awaited the pain to stop and then felt a raindrop.

Gotdamn it got damp.

A dark cloud reigned O her soul.

It was similar to the moment right before the confirmation cough of a coming cold. That heavy, overwhelming feeling that must exist in order to prepare for the sick storm ahead. Except she never coughed. She wasn't sick.

The young man released something inside of her. And whatever that something was wasn't going away.

Sex was the source. Intercourse is the deepest level of communication and it awakened a looming darkness. It's how evil finds itself by sniffing out and latching onto its victims through fornication.

Misery loves company.

For the moment, she thought they were making love. In his mind, it was just sex. There was no real emotion. Like most people, he didn't understand apathy is an emotion. Being unemotional is an emotion. And their emotions spilled onto each other when they spilled onto each other. He released his energy, and she gave him hers.

The feeling lasted weeks before intensifying. From Sunday to Sunday they had more sex and she felt more hexed. It was beyond a bad mood. It was a state she couldn't shake. She tried yoga, drew a bath, took a hot shower, smoked something, drank something and sat sweating in a sauna suffering to escape a shadow that lingered.

Nothing worked.

She couldn't kill it, so she buried it.

But burying death is like welcoming it home.

Gloom grew.

Her spirit darkened while the young man's became light. Tables turned like a DJ the way she spun the next moment.

"I think I'm in love!" He offered perfect words before the orgasm like most men do.

On all fours, she looked back at him awkwardly, followed by still silence. She didn't deign to discuss dittos.

"Thanks." She replied with a smirk. She was pulling a him on him as he pulled a fistful of her hair from behind.

The unforgiving young lady gave the baggage full of rejection and abandonment back to the young man who gave it back to her.

When it rains, it pours.

SPECIFICATION

"He looked into eyes void of emotion desperately trying to find something there. Anything. In a weird way, her mom was like a mother figure to him and he needed someone to mourn with. He searched for a connection in his neighbor, but she was cold as October."

The setting of the scene is somber. The mood is gray; the moment is confusing when we find out there is a repast occurring across the street from the young man's home. Everyone is in dark clothing, but the young lady wears a red sundress. She protests her emotions, putting on like she doesn't care and acting unaffected.

What the young woman doesn't realize is that she's exhibiting the same behavior as her mother. She's learning to be tough in complicated situations even if she's misunderstood through the process. She sacrifices emotion for the greater goal. This full-circle moment represents her mother's transition. What or where does she transition to?

That's for you to decide.

Meanwhile, his attempt to connect with his neighbor is met with resistance. He learns she connects better physically than verbally and there's good reason for that. Their love story started well, now they're having difficulty continuing the fairytale. They're not on the same page, though they've read the same books. He's vulnerable when she's guarded and he becomes guarded whenever she displays openness. They both want what doesn't want them. Something they learned to do a long time ago.

"She let him fuck deep inside because deep inside she didn't give a fuck."

Actually she did. Her mother–whom she never reconciled with– just died, and in the middle of it all, her neighbor–who she hadn't seen in years–popped up like an annoying Internet ad. She hates to feel anything, and as a result, goes through life not acknowledging the truth in front of her. She avoids reality by not reacting to it, leaving her emotions unresolved.

Sometimes sex is an escape.

Giving a fuck causes stress. She gave none. Her right hand slid into his jean pocket and felt for the curve. It's the only feeling she cared for. She was dependent on the antidote that caused her side effects. He was her headache and Advil – the problem and the fix. Each night he licked her wounds. He located lust on her labia, but no love. Sex was medicinal. It was the only place they connected, which amplified their disconnection. He was bad for her, but she needed him to break her so she could recognize what never to go back to.

The only time they could feel love was by making lust, so she did it often and he did it dangerously. Their guilty pleasure quickly turned into an unhealthy addiction.

Every thrust was an attempt to get back what she thought he stole from her. She was looking to heal from what hurt her. But she was searching in all the wrong places. He didn't steal anything. He continued her tradition of self-inflicted wounds. He shot from the ammo she gave him.

They say no one can drive you crazy unless you give up the key.

Let's keep it real, who are *they*, anyway? And aren't you sick of all their cute clichés that are easier said than done?

We're told to be in control of our emotions and no one can hurt us unless we allow it. Sounds good on paper, but isn't it impractical in person?

No.

If you're honest with yourself, you might find that you're not actually upset at all the people you've been pointing and flipping the finger at after all. When someone hurts you, do you ever sit with the feeling, reflect and think about why it caused you to get upset in the first place? I doubt it. But if you'd like to try, it will force you to face a flawed foundation. There's likely a single source that caused your anger and all your relationships are a manifestation of the pain you collected. If you're seriously hurt, it doesn't take much for emotion to rise. Everything agitates you. Anything annoys you. Even forgivable offenses serve as a reminder of your traumatic past. You get upset at little things. More often than not, we're not as angry at the person as we are about the resurfacing memory we'd like to forget. Yes, they're responsible for what they did, but they're not responsible for the way you react to it. Bitterness arrests time. When you make the decision to be unforgiving, you make the decision to carry the sins of your perpetrator. You survive, but you don't recover. You move on without healing and carry on the baggage like carry-on baggage. The weight remains with you on your journey. There, you'll find someone else to blame. To be unforgiving is to hold on. To forgive is to let go. Which is why forgiveness isn't just for the culprit, it is also for you.

There goes another of those cheap clichés we can all afford.

The agony of suffering is a torturous cycle when we don't forgive. Pain seeks more pain, so when you seek connections from a place of pain, you inevitably connect to pain. You attract what you are despite the masks you wear. It's how pretty people often attract ugly souls and end up suffering much heartbreak. Perfection is the armor that protects insecurity. Mostly all masks are rooted in fear. And deep down beneath your independence, ego and arrogance, you're a scared child who believes in your fears more than you believe in your truth. You fear being hurt, unworthy and unlovable. The truth is you're fearfully and wonderfully made. You're God's masterpiece. You're beloved. You're chosen. You're an overcomer. There is someone out there that you can undress for. Not clothing, but a removal of the masks you wear. Someone you won't have to hide yourself in front of. You won't have to be too perfect or dumb it down. You won't have to act so tough or be rude. You can show your quirks and idiosyncrasies that come with a guaranteed grin or their moment back. And that moment will be a time in your life you can finally live for yourself – for the moment.

But falsely projecting your truth doesn't protect you from pain – it shows how vulnerable you really are.

Be careful.

THE GRAY

Time doesn't heal all wounds. Neither does sex. Remember that thing about cheap clichés?

Drink some wine. Cry. Have another sip. Pray and get over it. You heal your own wounds when you decide to accept apologies from your past you may never receive.

Besides, it's foolish to hold grudges against people too busy living life to care. While you're pouting over three-year-old issues, they're somewhere in Italy in route to France with their three-year-old kid. They forgot you exist, and you've been mad at them for so long you forgot why you're mad at them.

You're stuck.

Time moved on, but you haven't.

You must identify the source of your pain – not just the symptoms.

GIVE YOURSELF PERMISSION TO FEEL

I wonder if a flower grows angry when it blooms. Does a caterpillar loathe its cocoon? We are the sole species to reject discomfort. There's value in suffering because discomfort develops us if we let it. Life won't always feel good. It's not designed to. Everything won't be OK and that's OK. Whatever you feel is OK because feelings foster growth when you let them. Strength is a byproduct of pain.

Expressing emotion isn't soft – it's hard because society says we can't do it.

Forget society.

From now on, you have full permission to express every instinctual feeling you feel, but please be adult about it. More specifically, be mature. Society says we can be afraid, disgusted, surprised, trusting and expecting. We're even allowed to laugh and express joy when a joke is funny, but we're not supposed to cry when we're sad. What part of the game is that? What do you think happens to sorrowful energy? It festers until it rots. Anger is often the result of mismanaged sadness. Hate is often the result of mismanaged love.

Remember that last sentence forever and you'll save yourself some headaches.

Allow yourself to feel, but don't dwell there. Don't let your feelings make you question your truth. Truth will remain truth whether pondered, accepted or denied. Get in and get out. Be angry, but don't go to bed upset. Awake with joy in the morning.

WEEP MORE

Women, let men cry.

You call for us to show more emotion so we show emotion and then you break up with us for being too emotional, get with another unemotional guy and the cycle continues. We assume responsibility for our patriarchal narrative, but accept the role you play as well.

Men, if you're not addressing problems, you have problems. You're supposed to feel your feelings and that's why they're called feelings.

Feelings should move you! They should help navigate your way. They show you where to go and when to stay. But we must acknowledge that they exist. Don't teach your sons that men don't cry. You'll ruin them. We have to get familiar with our feelings in order to manage them. At every stopping point along the way, it's important to ask, "How does this make me feel?" Your answer determines your direction. To think something is wrong with that means something is wrong with you.

Can I get an Amen?

Emotions are a response to life's moments whether good, bad, happy or sad. Feelings are a reflection of who we are when it matters most. Why would you hide that from anyone?

FEEL, HEAL AND MOVE ON

If you had to give up one of your five senses, which one would it be? I'd often ask myself this question as a child. My response was always my sense of touch. If I got rid of it, I could hold my finger under a lighter's flame longer. I could fall off of my bike without getting hurt. I'd be able to punch the kid who tried to beat me up on Ruby Avenue right in the jaw without feeling anything. Sounds good in theory, but if you can't feel pain, you don't even know you're hurt. Pain is the real teacher that taught me fire burns and destroys. Pain taught me how to maneuver a bike better than my parents could have ever taught me. Pain taught me that trusting God, not fighting, solves impossible problems.

There's beauty in being hurt.

The experience of pain shouldn't paralyze us; it should improve us. Pain lets us know what to do better next time. Pain is the vaccine that allows you to make it through your next attack. Embrace it. Hurt will heal you if you let it. That's why people say, "Confront your fears." Sometimes crying is a part of that process.

Tears are a natural release. Otherwise our bodies collectively wouldn't do it. Holding in tears is like holding in urine. Results could be damaging. Instead allow the drops to surface where you can see, feel and deal with them. Ultimately, you will understand them. If you don't address black and white issues, suppression turns them gray. And that's where many of us exist today.

You can suffocate your problems, but their ghosts will return to haunt you. It's how an abused child becomes an abusive parent. It's how rape replaces innocence with perversion in its victims. It's how relationships stay stale like a bag of chips you failed to properly close. Crying is the start of closure. Tears are a sign of confession and can be the first steps toward healing.

I don't trust people who don't cry.

If you cried more, maybe you wouldn't drink as often. Maybe you wouldn't smoke as much and pop as many prescription pills. Perhaps you wouldn't ceaselessly seek escapades and affairs. Maybe you wouldn't work so much or be as busy. Run toward your fears and not away from them. Run toward pain and you'll eventually pass it gaining strength, confidence and audacity in route.

Set your suffering free and weep for weeks, days or only seconds as long as you let go. Numbing your troubles only increases your problems. The longer you keep the contaminant in, the more it'll eat at you. Misery is like bacteria that reduces your level of strength, activity and desire until your will is weak. Once in a depressed state, you're easier to control.

"Controlled by what?" You ask.

Well, by something viler, more sinister and more threatening. It'll take you down deep to a dark place where there is no future. No answer. There is no light. No hope. Only sorrow. Nothing is enjoyable. Nothing makes you smile. You're just falling. Falling so far you no longer know the source of the perpetual sadness. It's the only thing you feel. All else is numb. Nothing tastes, smells, sounds or feels familiar except unhappiness.

Some of us know this place all too well.

Others are skilled at concealing emotional trauma. We don't go down as easily. Trouble has taught us how to forget. Inspiration has motivated us to move on. So we believe we've transitioned our pain into our purpose. We're hardworking and tenacious. We put our heads down and got laser focused. And when we looked up, we amassed so much success that we don't even know our next-door neighbors. They live too far across the street to see. You have a nice home and beautiful family, but you're no different than everyone else. There's a mess inside of you so complicated, with all your knowledge, you can't even figure it out.

You have to ask yourself, why you didn't deal with a problem as soon as it became a problem. Was it out of embarrassment or fear? Ask yourself why you were afraid or embarrassed? Keep digging because your truth is at the end of the most difficult question. Maybe it happened during a period you were unable to understand or digest. You must revisit your era of emotional trauma and sit there. Remain until a resolution is reached. It's going to get uncomfortable. It's going to hurt like hell.

Stay there.

I'll wait.

The more you feel, the closer you are. Cry so much that your face may never dry. Cry in the morning and plan to cry again at night.

Let it rain.

"No doubt the divorce caused a rift in their relationship. Every child needs a little extra love and she probably felt abandoned during the division. She was part of the divorce too. Her mother was too consumed to notice."

Children who experience unresolved trauma often mature physically, but not emotionally. Eventually they become adults. Unsettled damage creates secret scars. She's older, but the spirit of a hurt little girl remains inside of her. It never got to grow when she did.

Can you relate?

Has anything stunted your growth?

"For the moment she thought they were making love. In his mind, it was just sex. There was no real emotion. Like most people, he didn't understand apathy is an emotion. Being unemotional is an emotion. And their emotions spilled onto each other when they spilled onto each other. He released his energy and she gave him hers."

Sex is the exchange of information. When a man has sex with a woman, he not only enters her body, he goes into her innermost being and attaches himself to all that exists there. When a woman has sex with a man, she is taking in all that he is by receiving his inner most energy. When you release all that you know and all that you are with someone who is releasing all they know and all they are – the meaningful exchange is enough to create life. Sex is marriage. Marriage is sex. It's the deepest connection you can ever have with someone. And if you go deep enough, you'll meet God.

So do you really think you can leave the interaction unaffected?

The first law of thermodynamics states that energy is neither created nor destroyed; rather, it transfers or transforms from one form to another.

Sex is an emotional exchange of energy. Still, there are men that claim they can have sex with no emotion. But having no emotion is an emotion. Indifference is an emotion. Not caring is an emotion. And all that negative energy is spread through intercourse.

Having sex is the most available you can make yourself. The connection spreads your purest, most honest and raw energy. If you don't believe emotions are transferable, how do you explain why being around happy people makes you happy? Or how being around negativity puts you in a dark mood? Think about method actors and how they become haunted by, and often suffer from the emotions of the characters they play. Think of emotions as a cloud that lingers around like Pigpen from *Peanuts*. If you come in contact with the fog, it attaches to you.

Perhaps the next time your emotional booty call texts you, "Hey stranger," at 2:01 a.m. after a bad day, you can ask where he or she plans on unloading all that depression!

OCTOBER

OCTOBER // MASSACRE

S he drew a bath, opened her legs immediately under the faucet and let her thoughts run with the water. It was a ritual she practiced religiously.

She was 19 now. He was 23.

Their union was gray. Some days she was his girlfriend – some days she was his girl friend. That single space in the word created space in their relationship that made her feel single. At times she felt like an ex because she was never introduced as anything more than a friend.

So she stopped calling to see who kept in touch. He didn't. She started missing his calls, but didn't miss his touch. She realized as a grown woman she should never have to sit and question if a grown man is interested in her. When a gentleman is interested, he maneuvers mountains to get what he wants.

He wouldn't even send a text.

Then like a stroke of luck sent from a blue genie on a magical carpet, it came.

"Hey..."

She was excited, but planned to take her sweet time responding back. Besides, "Hey," isn't a question or comment, and he didn't seem concerned.

She convinced herself she didn't care. She told herself not to care. She tried not to. But in reality, she did.

"What kind of woman do you think I am?? You reach out when it's convenient for you and I'm supposed to drop everything to respond to your one-word, three-letter message. I'm not the text you 100 times type, I'm the I've got options type. You need to learn to court if you wanna lay-up…"

She smirked as she typed. She was pleased with her wit. She was satisfied with her insistence – but she didn't press send. She responded to his message, but she didn't send it. She wanted him to know how it felt to burn awaiting a response. She needed to feel desired even if only for fifteen minutes. So she let her draft sit like a coach does an injured rookie.

Furthermore, she felt connected by having in-person experiences, sharing stories and openly expressing emotion. Not a text message.

She was torn and he was her cheap bandage – temporary and good enough for now, until falling off.

"Guess who's been on my mind…"

His allusion was an illusion that caused elusion.

"…"

He awaited a finished sentence, but it remained incomplete – just like them. She refused to address the issues, and he was left to assume the answers. Their relationship was an ellipsis – a hint with no conclusion. They spoke often, but rarely communicated. They knew of each other, but didn't really know each other.

They were never specific and never direct. She expected to be understood without an instruction manual. He expected to get what he wanted without giving her what she needed.

She's comfortable with confusion. They don't go on dates; they go on distractions. They need each other to divert each other though they pretend they need each other. It helps them cope with secret misery. I wish someone told her the photos she posted to her profile of people popping the question probably wouldn't inspire him to propose. He doesn't even visit her page.

So she sent a final farewell and they agreed to meet for the very last time. Like an Uber, his *ex* arrived better than expected. The minute he saw her, was the second he knew. It was obvious. She knew and she knew that he knew. She was aware of how her body overtook that dress and she wore it on purpose. She told him…she said, "I feel sorry for her."

"Who?" He said.

"The woman you experience after this…"

It happened that way in her head, but not in actuality.

She was superwoman in her mind, but more like Lois Lane in real life.

She and her superman were sort of like post-high school sweethearts. Now here's the not-so-sweet part. They spent weeks apart. And here's the weakest part – her contractions were contracting barely beats a part. He was in the studio. Tearing beats apart. You wouldn't think he had a heartbeat how he beat her heart. Love ends. People part. But you never thought that this would be the part where she won't return. The dope will burn. Possessions earned. Lesson learned.

The genesis of their relationship contained a revelation they ignored.

It was finished before it started.

She was irritable when they first met in her driveway and wasn't changing anytime soon.

They broke up often like young couples do.

Then got back together like young couples do.

They were off and on like a toddler discovering a light switch for the first time. For the first time in a long time they hadn't talked in a while. Two weeks feels like a month when you're young. Autumn lasts half the year.

Still, they held on.

The doctor said she was having a baby. But fate would have it otherwise.

Blood soaked. Blood soiled. Blood smeared. Her boyfriend made it to the hospital in time for the news.

Stillbirth.

It's scary when you miscarry. A blur of blue and white coats and masks is all you remember. And confusion. Chaos and panic packaged as routine procedure.

It was the worst thing that ever happened to her. It was worse than violation and abandonment. It was worse than her worst moment multiplied by your worst moment. At least that's how it felt.

"He's innocent! He's innocent! He's just a baby…"

Her words were like knives cutting everyone in the room revealing their humanity. Awful screams stained hospital walls. She bellowed in agony in a pitch only a mourning mother knows how to sing.

Doctors deal with expiration daily, but this was different. It was difficult. A little girl lost a little boy – something she'd dealt with before, but unlike this. And a mother lost a child – something she could relate to, but unlike this.

Days passed and the results came in. The medical examiner found traces of cocaine in the baby's system.

The young woman partied with blow a few times, but nothing heavy. She'd cut a few lines to get in a few parties and cut a few lines at a few parties. She celebrated a birthday. She was almost a woman.

THE GRAY

Beautiful. And young.

She never thought a few flat lines would cause her fetus to flatline. It's how one decision affects everything. And everything.

Death is a loud wake up call.

"Good morning." The doctor woke her up early the next day.

Exhaustion and heavy medication had her out. She took a quick assessment of the room as if checking to make sure it was all just a terrible dream. It wasn't. This time, it was for real.

Her boyfriend was still sitting in the same chair he'd sat in since he sat down the first day. He hadn't said much except to see if she needed anything and assured her everything would be OK. He was always there for her in the moments that mattered most.

Two deaths.

Well, three.

The death of her mother;

The death of their son;

And the death of her.

She let her eyelids shut again. It was safer in her sleep. He stayed up and watched her rest. Her breath was rhythmic – almost an album. She snored, but to him it was beautiful.

Every part of her was.

She was 21 when she grew conscious. He was 25. Depression feels like a long, slow slumber. Two years went by without her realizing it. Denial freezes time. Some days she slept for some days. Sunday was just some day. Friday was just like Monday. She wasn't alert. She was just there.

And so was he.

His loyalty was unquestionable. He made sure she ate at least three meals a day and did the dishes. He bathed her when she couldn't gather the strength to do so on her own. He produced a playlist full of her favorite songs to play during difficult days. He washed her face. He brushed her hair and wrapped it up in a headscarf before bed. He never once left her side. Tragedy will make you view life differently in that way.

October matured the man when his son went down.

He was done playing games. He didn't want to pretend he didn't like her for the glory of the chase. He didn't feel like waiting hours before replying to her messages to make it seem like she wasn't important. He didn't want to do or say anything to try and make her jealous or trigger a reaction. Like a cow flushing the toilet, he was done with the bullshit. He believed in chemistry and energy, but science isn't a sign.

"Let's do this for real or not at all." He blurted matter-of-factly.

"Excuse me?" She gave him her attention.

"Let's forget about punctuation and sentence structure. Let's ignore commas and periods. We're like one run-on sentence. We're a mess. But you're my mess."

"We're complex."

He continued.

"When you just stop. And think about it. Despite it all, life is good."

He had a way with words. He knew how to say the right things to make her believe. It's how he got her attention in the first place.

"Our life is our life. It could be better, and I've got plans to make it better. But I can't do it without you. You're my bridge to God. With you, I know my flaws because you make me see myself. I want to be the best me because of you. I need you like I need God. And the three of us, we can take over the world. So let's get married."

Her mouth opened, but no words fell out.

She didn't want to waste words. Words fail to deliver accuracy. Sometimes sentences tell underwhelming stories that aren't touching enough for a recipient of remarks to feel. What is said can be questioned. What is done cannot.

She didn't say yes with her mouth – she said it with her movement.

She didn't say I love you with her words – she said it with her mouth.

She started addressing him by undressing him with her tongue against his neckline and her teeth on his T-shirt.

Interpretations taint firsthand accounts so I'll say it like he saw it:

This woman wasn't an option, she was an opportunity – and he had an option to take this opportunity to acknowledge her as such. This was his moment to show her she's amazing, but sometimes amazing is just a cheap word for god. She was other like a deity. She wasn't born, she was sent. She wasn't of earth, but out of this world and he was fortunate to have her. Genuflect in the presence of greatness. And kiss her while you're down there.

He did. He pressed his nose against her naval with both eyes closed, allowing her scent to lure him down even further. A deep inhale let him know who she was. She was the one. Her taste was foreign like something he'd never had. No funny fishy fragrance or odd odor, only an ambrosial aroma and a fistful of ass. She was about to get all his free will.

He kissed the color from her lips – all four of them.

He wanted to inhale her. He wanted his actuality in her mouth. He didn't want to screw her. He wanted to climb inside of her, find himself and then show her who he was. He needed her to feel his truth. He made love like he missed her. Like he hadn't seen her in years. He hadn't. He was raw in. She was riding. He was all in. She was sliding. He was wide in. She said Amen.

Dear God,

It was the greatest quickie in the history of man. Five senses satisfied in four minutes.

Mind blown.

Literally.

Figuratively.

Both.

All.

At the end of the day when was all said and done, she needed love. She didn't care what it looked like. It didn't have to come with a ribbon tied around it. It didn't have a height or weight requirement. She didn't want what was perfect. She wanted a willing participant. She needed to see someone love her through her mess so she knew she was possible to love. It wasn't the advice in the books she read, but it was her truth. She's not a segment, section, a piece or percentage. She's whole. She's entire. She comes complete. Which means she comes complicated. He couldn't love her sass without tolerating her attitude in the a.m. He couldn't honor her body without admiring her beautiful brain. She had to stop running and let life happen naturally. She wasn't improving over night. She was like wine and that takes time to refine.

Speaking of wine, let's take a break to pour some. That sex scene was beautiful!

Seriously, have a glass and get comfortable.

I'll wait.

Now raise your glass for this next scene...

He couldn't wait to make an honest woman out of her. They went to the courthouse the next morning and made it official.

Some people call it marriage – some people call it a massacre.

"Till death do us part."

Cheers.

SPECIFICATION

"Their union was gray. Some days she was his girlfriend – some days she was his girl friend. That single space in the word created space in their relationship that made her feel single."

UNCLEAR INTENTIONS ARE CLEAR INTENTIONS THAT YOU HAVE NO INTENTIONS

If you actually have intentions, but the timing is off, then say that. If you're not where you want to be, then say so. If you're scared to commit, address it. Just don't leave someone hanging due to indecision. Give people the opportunity to decide if they want to work through it or give you space. In partnerships there's negotiation. Learn joint decision-making by communicating through uncertainty.

State your intentions when your intentions become your intentions.

Clear intention fosters hope. It clears the pathway to envision a future that both of you can agree on. It allows you to track progress and manage deliverables instead of wishing upon a star that someone might dare make a move.

Don't move!

Stay right there, grab your phone and snap a picture of this page. Upload it to social media and tag @bereolaesque. Together, we'll get through this. I'm holding you accountable for never allowing yourself to be an option because you're actually an opportunity. Don't be an unmarried wife. "Almost engaged" is code word for permanent girlfriend. I guess that's like being sort of pregnant? Don't accept bird behavior to avoid ruffling feathers. What about your feathers? You want to fly too! Life is about progression. Demand legitimacy. Don't be afraid to ask questions. If questions ruin it, then it was already ruined before it began. You did yourself a favor. Do yourself a favor and thank me later.

To the Men who won't Promote Her:

I've seen people go from intern to executive in ten years – meanwhile she's still your girlfriend. She's your lifetime fiancée. You entered your relationship with no goals and no plan like a college senior still in General Studies. There is no graduation. You don't need a wristwatch to know what time it is. It's time to have the talk, or walk. The choice is yours. And if she starts off with, "We need to talk," just talk. Don't critique her approach and create a separate argument from the original problem so you don't have to deal with her questions. Now you forgot what you're arguing about. It's time to get on the same page because you obviously haven't read my book.

Why'd you approach her in the first place? You sold her a dream and now you're holding her hostage from the community. She's living a nightmare with you as her oppressor.

Free her – then free yourself!

Women wear strength like clothing, but love penetrates the armor. Her inner workings of intricate workmanship are precious. When a woman reveals herself to expose her truth, it's going to take someone real to protect that

Listen, next time you notice a strong woman with a great career, financial independence and sex appeal on another level and you're still out there trying to figure out where you want to be, leave her be. Admire her from afar. Don't approach her when you're trying to be – approach her when you are. Don't go ruining it by getting her contact information, manipulating her to fall for you, breaking her spirit and leading her to conclude that all guys are the same.

Just let her be dope.

Alone.

I hope we've reached an agreement.

"So she stopped calling to see who kept in touch. He didn't. She started missing his calls, but didn't miss his touch. She realized as a grown woman she should never have to sit and question if a grown man is interested in her. When a gentleman is interested, he maneuvers mountains to get what he wants."

But you surely can't lift a mountain if you can't lift a phone.

This is usually how the story goes:

You ignore her presence so now you feel her absence. She was cute enough to kick it, but not interesting enough to pursue. You had your shot, but you shot yourself in the foot. That's not a pimp-walk – it's a limp, and your go-to crutch is, "Money over Bitches," though you lack both.

She misses you, but she doesn't want you.

Why didn't you pay attention when she did? Attention is free. Why didn't you continue to do what you did to get her once you had her? Why are you interested now that she's not interested in you? Now, you suddenly wonder. Now, you have time. Now, she suddenly matters.

But you don't.

It's too late.

Let me know if that sounds about right. Next, let me know if this behavioral pattern makes any damn sense at all.

"She was torn and he was her cheap bandage – temporary and good enough for now until falling off."

Listen, your singlehood is sacred. It's a birthright. Why are people giving it up so easily? It should be a privilege for anyone to take that from you. Cling onto it until someone deemed worthy is able to snatch your single like Aubrey featured on any artist's songs.

I get it. It seems like everyone has someone and that can heighten your awareness of solitude – especially during the holidays. Your judgment is off and patience is low. Your bed is cold and your batteries are dead, so you connect with someone deplorable. You realize this and find another sorry replacement. It's what you do. You feel unlovable so you don't love yourself and find a man happy to treat you how you treat yourself. The sick cycle continues.

Being single is only depressing if you are. A relationship won't change that. Your significance isn't dependent on a significant other. Having one isn't the prize – you are. Since your first breath you've been relevant and will remain so even when you try to convince yourself otherwise.

There's so much more in life to connect with other than a wrinkled penis or soggy vagina. Discover more. Do more. Be more. The world will respond to you when you decide you are greater.

Running from alone is a dangerous race. I hope you lose.

"So she sent a final farewell and they agreed to meet for the very last time."

Why must we always set up a final send-off meeting? It's like an alcoholic saying, "One last shot!" What is being accomplished by meeting in person? Is it your display of etiquette and respect? You can be cordial via email. Don't say you're leaving just to be cute, elicit a response and renegotiate. Say you're leaving because you aren't coming back. You don't negotiate with terrorists!

I swear you don't want this feeling. The feeling isn't fleeting. It won't subside. It isn't going away. You think you've moved on, but emotions linger and resurface too frequently for comfort like flatulence in an elevator.

Songs, scents and sloppy sex scenes on sitcoms still serve as reminders. The memories can't be washed. You don't want to care, but you do. You try not to think about it, but you do. It's ever-present. It's there. It's real … until you put your phone down.

Block.

Delete.

Erase.

Celebrate!

Please, put your phone down. And celebrate responsibly!

"The genesis of their relationship was a revelation they ignored."

I'm sure you can relate. I know I can.

I've entered relationships that were solely based on physical attraction hoping we'd figure it out along the way. We didn't. It never worked out because our foundation was baseless. There was nothing there.

Usually there is something there – like warning signs advising us to proceed with caution or lights flashing, "Do Not Enter." But we ignore signs when the sex is good. She ignored the signs when he texted her, "Good morning, love." Though she knew better, she needed to feel better. There was a lot on her plate and sometimes a girl just wants to go out on a dope date, be treated like a lady, then come home and get her hair pulled.

Every day.

At the end of the day, if you wouldn't be friends outside of the relationship, you don't belong in the relationship. And that's the best way to determine if you need to end the relationship. Otherwise, we find every reason to justify staying together. "My mother loves him." "He's going through a tough time – I can't leave him now." "I never thought I'd have a woman like this – I can't let her go." "We've been together too long to just give up now. If nothing changes in a year, I'll reevaluate."

You said the same thing last year.

Some New Year's resolutions have to start right now.

"A little girl lost a little boy – something she'd dealt with before, but unlike this. And a mother lost a child – something she could relate to, but unlike this."

This supreme sentence reveals the depth of the young woman's suffering. She's fragile, but doesn't break. Maybe she needs to break so she can properly heal. She routinely reveals strength amidst adversity. This paramount moment is a breaking point and turning point for her. She faces figurative and literal loss. She lost the boy she fell for fast when he took her innocence. And she loses her only begotten son. She relates to her mother who also loses a child when she passes on from cancer. But her mother is gone and her child is still here. In this instance, a mother is still here, but her child is gone.

He hadn't said much except to see if she needed anything and assured her everything would be OK. He was there for her in the moments that mattered most in her life.

Two deaths.

Well, three.

The death of her mother;

The death of their son;

And the death of her."

Her spirit died a long time ago.

"October matured the man when his son went down."

This sentence has dual meaning, as the word "son" is a homophone for the word "sun." October is the month his son goes down into the ground for burial. The experience eternally changes him.

When the sun goes down in the month of October, it gets cold. We respond to temperature change. The woman was his sun. She was his dawn and afternoon light that provided inspiration and energy in his life. She was hot, and at times unbearable, but perfect when warm. And when she went down, he stepped up. He recognized that he needed her and she needed him. It was the moment he knew he had something in his life he wanted forever.

"He was done playing games. He didn't want to pretend he didn't like her for the glory of the chase. He didn't feel like waiting hours before replying to her messages to make it seem like she wasn't important. He didn't want to do or say anything to try and make her jealous or trigger a reaction. Like a cow flushing the toilet, he was done with the bullshit."

More than likely, when a man masquerades around like he doesn't care, he's actually showing that he does. He pretends to be preoccupied. He acts like his options are options. He knows you're the one when he unjustifiably resists you.

You flood his thoughts because his mental dam doesn't give a damn. He tries convincing himself he's too busy because he's too afraid. He's afraid of the possibilities. He's afraid to be great. He feels like there has to be a perfect moment. He thinks his money has to be right and all things have to be in place before taking that next beautiful step.

Teach him that he doesn't have to have it all together. You'll accept him broken because you're broken. Be willing to pick up where he left off if he's willing to make the same promise. He's joining a team. It won't just be him out there all alone. It'd be the both of you. He'll learn he doesn't have to make every one of his dreams come true first. You'll make them come true together.

"She didn't say yes with her mouth – she said it with her movement. She didn't say I love you with her words – she said it with her mouth."

Simplicity is a Universal Language

Communication is a woman's Native tongue. Sex is the ultimate conversation.

Nothing more needs to be said.

"It was a massacre.

Some people call it marriage."

The third chapter marries them. I'm sure you didn't expect it. I know I didn't. The chapter begins with hopelessness and ends in hope.

Well, doesn't it?

INTERLUDE
Evacuation Plan

GOING GRAY

You might be in a gray area if:

- You have to ask, "So, what are we?" after putting the tip in.

- You date the person you're "dating" only when dinner is involved.

- You're embarrassed to admit to ten years when asked how long you've been seeing each other.

- You ask everyone else about your relationship except the person you're in a relationship with.

- You have an HTML romance – text only.

- You haven't met his wife.

- You're on a constant search to find something wrong with the person you're with.

- You're uncomfortable discussing finances.

- You anticipate hearing, "Maybe" or "I'll let you know" when texting, "I want to see you."

- You're told that marriage is just a piece of paper.

- Your friends still think you're single.

- You have to check social media to find out your relationship status.

- You agree to the terms of a trial-based and commitment-free relationship, only to realize you've been paying the price for your time, energy and effort the whole time.

- You're a serial monogamist.

- You're afraid to date.

- You believe love hurts. It doesn't. People do.

- You still think love hurts after reading the sentence above. People are flawed by nature, but love is pure. Getting hurt is just an example of someone failing to get love right.

- You can't look the person you love in the eye and tell your truth.

Prevention and practice before disaster: Store your book in safekeeping where it's quickly accessible. Have a plan in place and know where you can seek immediate shelter. Conduct practice drills on dates by uncovering intentions. This can be accomplished tactfully by inquiring what your date is looking to get out of the dating process.

Don't rely on forecasting: Forecasting isn't perfect and uncertainties do occur without warning. There is no substitute for staying alert.

Denial is the greatest danger: Know when you're in a gray area. Know when it's safe to stay and when you must evacuate.

After the disaster: Carefully render aid to the injured with this text.

NOVEMBER

November // Noir

Hormones were raging like Oakland wildfires. That's what honeymoons are for. Theirs was modest. No oceanfront suite, but plenty of waves.

Due to inclement weather conditions, they remained in bed.

Drip.

Drop.

Leak.

Puddles came suddenly. No forecast. No announcement – just a relentless flow of moisture. Due to no protection, he went inside. And inside was better than on top.

There was no etiquette. They had no morals.

Morality is doing what's right regardless of what you're told.

Obedience is doing what you're told regardless of what's right.

This was obedience.

There was a slight neck grip followed by an authoritative command.

"Bend down."

She did not come to play with him.

Bitch, she came to slay.

There were handcuffs, but no arrests.

His hands locked around her ankles where his lips gave her troubles a rest.

She felt something coming and didn't want progress to arrest.

Tongue's caress caused shortness of breath like cardiac arrest.

When she said, "Don't stop." He listened.

When she said, "I've arrived." He didn't listen.

Once more into the fray…

She satisfied his insatiable desire to discover more of her.

She fixed her jaws to beg, but he anticipated her request. He understood her enough to take the words from her mouth with his tongue, rendering her speechless.

He wanted to kiss her for a week.

Every hour.

Twenty-four times a day.

Mouths collapsed onto bodies and she tasted like deliverance. Her lips were 5-star resort pillows. French kisses were an international sojourn. Their bed was an island where she was floating in her own body of water.

Foreplay was just for play.

Her turn.

She wasn't going to chase what was already hers. She was going to take it. Her curious eyes drew him in like art.

Where do I even start?

Let's skip to the good part.

She liked him hard enough to penetrate beyond her walls, but soft enough to feel something. She wanted passion. She wanted some emotion. She wanted that exciting, teary-eyed, spiritual, fervent, fiery feeling to come just as she did.

Enough wasn't enough. Too long was too short. He took ownership over her moments. She was no longer in control. Her body became possessed by every stroke of genius. She almost had a stroke the way he had her body leaning.

The way he had her cervix singing was beautiful poetry. He was a gifted producer.

"You don't have to be delicate." She turned around and whispered.

He wasn't.

Sex should never be silent.

It wasn't.

They made love for an entire chapter.

And that was that.

SPECIFICATION

This chapter requires no interpretation.

Marriage is the safest space for woman and man to explore each other, every last drip and drop of their sexual desires, curiosities and fantasies.

For Judgmental Gentlemen:

Support a woman being a woman – no matter what the hell that looks like.

She keeps weed in her Chanel clutch. Merlot drips from her lips. Her degrees don't satisfy her because she's searching. She'll be at a club tonight and church tomorrow. She's searching. She's smarter than she lets on. She knows that the more she knows, the more she knows that she doesn't know much. And she wants you to know that she's not here for you to judge. If you can't figure her out, imagine how tough her job is. Don't take it personally – sometimes she doesn't even know why she's feeling down, insecure or emotional. She's strong. She's delicate. She's evolving. She's a woman. That's it. And that's enough. Either love her, or leave her alone.

FYI: She doesn't care what you think of her – she doesn't think of you at all.

NINETEENTH OF DECEMBER

Nineteenth Of December // Buyer's Remorse

R eal estate was cheap. He was making plans to build her a home in the sky and change her address to cloud nine. She couldn't see clearly with her head in the clouds, but she'd enjoy the pedestal. He would surprise her with a happy wife starter kit: a little dog and a big purse.

She could post it online.

She loved him.

Love like a river wide with no borders and depth unknown, as far as the eyes could see. Love that washes away and forever flows. Abundant love … until it touches land. Then it dries up.

That's how she loved him – until she touched land. When her high came down, she momentarily reconsidered it all. His eyes no longer illuminated her space like a light bill unpaid. Attention was unpaid. At times, she wanted to be gone like the river.

She was a serial commitment killer who bailed on relationships right before the six-month mark. Her mother died about six months after her sixteenth birthday. She didn't deal with the pain. Life taught her that everything is temporary. Pain was the only thing that was loyal to her. Pain is what she sought, and pain is what she got. She learned to miss people without wanting them. She stayed away from everything beautiful, anything nurturing and everyone who loved her. Love was too perfect to have it suddenly snatched away, so she gave it an expiration date.

She found balance in the gray area. It's how she handled love. She'd take it and give it back – then look for it again, only to give it back. There was no commitment in the gray. She hated that, but she loved him. He loved her, but he hated love. They were searching, but didn't know what they were searching for. They acknowledged their thirst and drank from a void source. It kept them parched.

He's too busy.

It was fun in the beginning. She admired his ambition, but lately there's been a battle for time and she's losing. When his presence wasn't felt, presents helped, but not any longer. She gets that he has to sacrifice time in order to get time, but when will she get her time?

"Is that you, baby?"

He needs more time.

She needs more of him.

She was waiting.

She waited.

She's fading.

It was all good just a week ago.

They say it takes two years for the honeymoon phase to fade. Perhaps they forgot to divide by four and carry the one day that a spark is no longer enough to ignite a flame.

For the first few months, their new union was like their old one when they first met. She had restored excitement for him and their future together.

"Baby, is that you downstairs?"

She called him hubby for the first few weeks, but the name didn't stick around.

Neither did he.

Winter's work kept him away. The season was a busy time of year for their little family. She was often left home alone where every gust of winter's wind knocking at the door reminded her of her husband's hard-bottom shoes hitting the hardwood.

It was cold in that house. She could've used some hard wood at that moment, but the only wood in their home was firewood. She started a small flame to warm up the place. Her husband was expected back from his work studio soon.

Whether a home is 500 square feet or 5,000 square feet, loneliness is still the same.

Marriage encouraged the woman to make unspoken sacrifices. She did all the thankless things for her husband that came without acknowledgment, but would be noticeable if she stopped doing them.

Pay attention.

Even though he was an ass earlier in morning, she left out a warm plate of food for him before heading out to work. She'd turn to his favorite channel before turning off the TV so all he had to do was turn it on when prepared to watch his shows. He gave her an unearned argument the other night, and she gave him some unearned ass before bed. While he showers, she put his towel in the dryer because she knows how much he dislikes the cold when stepping out.

I hope you're paying attention.

She loved him so she allowed him to be. She hated his sin, but she adored him, so she gave him room to grow. She didn't leave him when he was unfaithful. She saw the good in him and knew there was a chance he'd slip up before she said yes. She was a realist. She knew how handsome, immature and social he was when they met. Going cold turkey because he was with her was unrealistic. She let him fail in love with her, then fall in love with her. Only her. And he did.

Her kindness toward him wasn't based on who he was, but based on who she was becoming. She did what he didn't deserve. That's what grace is. She displayed her love for him by how much she sacrificed for him. It was her version of "ride or die," but she was no fool.

She was woman.

And she loved who she was becoming.

She made her decision and accepted her fate. Someone; something so undeniable came along into her life at a point when her heart wasn't ready, but she said F the rules. She accepted love, and marriage and all that came along with it. There was joy, and there was pain. That's what it was. That's what love is when filtered through the flawed vessel of humanity. She wasn't going to complain now. She was going to push through the difficulties and love him anyway.

And that's what she did.

Though there were one hundred reasons to give up, she found just one reason to hold on.

Love.

SPECIFICATION

"She loved him.

Love like a river wide with no borders and depth unknown, as far as the eyes could see. Love that washes away and forever flows. Abundant love ... until it touches land. Then it dries up."

This is beautiful because this is love. It has no limits or edges. But if you happen to fall in and your heart breaks, you didn't waste your time. You're not broken because you loved and lost. In fact you are greater because you were bold enough to stand strong, face it and get through it. You landed in love. And stood there. That's what love does. That's what love is.

You will fall out of like. Don't panic.

It won't always be champagne and orange juice. Emotions come and go. No one is sexy during arguments and mimosas don't fix everything. Jokes stop being funny, happiness seems distant and you're not into it anymore.

But that's your baby and you find your way back to that joyous place.

This isn't the time to give up. It's the time to put in work. There will be times when your partner is weak and you must compensate and love harder. There will be times when you're weak and your partner has to be strong for the both of you. Decide to love even when you don't feel loved. Be intentional even when it's not deserved. It's not easy – it's a relationship. And any relationship that lasts long enough will be tested. Nothing worth it will be perfect, but anything worth it is worth fighting for.

I hope you know the difference.

"She found balance in the gray area. It's how she handled love. She'd take it and give it back – then look for it again, only to give it back. There was no commitment in the gray. She hated that, but she loved him. He loved her, but he hated love. They were searching, but didn't know what they were searching for. They acknowledged their thirst and drank from a void source. It kept them parched."

If I got water from a dirty well, I wouldn't lose hope in water – I'd lose hope in the well. So why are you out here with lost hope in love because you lost hope in a person? Love is channeled through dirty vessels we call human beings. It's only when we are connected to love that it is able to flow through us without blemish.

God is love.

Know the difference.

"He's too busy.

It was fun in the beginning. She admired his ambition, but lately there's been a battle for time and she's losing. When his presence wasn't felt, presents helped, but not any longer. She gets that he has to sacrifice time in order to get time, but when will she get her time?"

Gender roles can lead to gray areas. Most men in a relationship are expected to be the breadwinner. This supports the idea that we are supposed to be the leader of our household by financially providing. However, with women breaking barriers and experiencing a sense of equality, they're becoming the family's financial support – and rightfully so. In other scenarios, the man makes the most money, but the woman is more responsible, organized and knowledgeable with it. In both examples, honoring gender roles can force couples into making bad decisions. Some believe so strongly in them, they're willing to bypass everything that makes sense to honor a role. They didn't get honor roll in school.

We must get out of this backwards way of thinking in relationships. They wouldn't make a man who's terrible at finance the CFO in Corporate America just because he has a penis. So why are men running around in relationships feeling obligated to run the money? And why are so many women letting us?

Addressing an obvious problem is never as bad as ignoring one. You wonder why he isn't talking to you when you come home from work? Probably because his job isn't working and no one wants to talk about what it's doing to the relationship. Feelings of dissatisfaction and discouragement go undiscussed and disgust sets in. He feels inadequate and takes his frustrations out on you with an ever present silent attitude that he denies when you ask what's wrong. But you know what's wrong. And it's time to talk about it before more fights about nothing reoccur.

Relationship are about adopting what's best in a person and applying it to make you better. In exchange you offer the best of you in hopes of making them better. It's a mutually beneficial connection that requires you to always aim for greatness.

Among many things, my wife is incredible at organizing activities on our vacations. Leave it up to me, and we'll stay at the resort's pool all week. But she plans all of these amazing excursions, activities and seeks out the best restaurants for the trip. It's like a vacation within a vacation. So why would I let my ego impede on what she's good at? It doesn't mean I don't try to get better at planning vacations so she can experience a dope surprise every once in a while, but I want her to be great at what she's good at. And she lets me handle the things in our relationship that I'm the best at doing. It just makes sense.

If you're tired of doing everything in your relationships because you're better at everything, then stop dating losers. Or maybe you're the loser – too controlling. Give good people the opportunity to be great. We all need to feel needed.

"Her kindness toward him wasn't based on who he was, but based on who she was becoming. She did what he didn't deserve. That's what grace is. She displayed her love for him by how much she sacrificed for him. It was her version of "ride or die," but she was no fool.

She was woman.

And she loved who she was becoming."

A wise woman gives an incompetent man the illusion of power while she subtly sits back and maintains it. She tames his demons. She balances his masculinity. She knows when to feed the ego and when to starve it because she knows him well enough to know which situations he responds best in. She secretly steers their ship with seduction, grace and femininity – irresistible to most men. She's not only empowered to voice her opinion, but to navigate the connection. A man needs a woman to make him better. A better husband. A better son. A better father. And a better man.

Balance.

Recognize a good one before he or she is gone.

"She made her decision and accepted her fate. Someone; something so undeniable came along in her life at a point when her heart wasn't ready, but she said F the rules. She accepted love, and marriage and all that came along with. There was joy, and there was pain, and that's what it was. That's what love is when filtered through the flawed vessel of humanity. She wasn't going to complain now. She was going to push through the difficulties and love him anyway.

And that's what she did."

TO BE LOVED IS EASY – TO LOVE IS A MOTHERF'ER

She didn't want a convenient lover. Love isn't supposed to be convenient. Love is an inconvenient choice – one that demands tough decisions and unpopular settlements. She wanted her relationship to reveal her flaws and challenge her to grow. She accepted love as inconvenient and loved him still because she's learning that's how connections work best. It won't be all good at all times, but you commit to being good in bad times and that's what makes it good.

TO LOVE IS EASY – TO BE LOVED IS A MOTHERF'ER

Loving him was teaching her to love herself. She just wanted a cure, an escape, anything that would allow her to heal and finally learn to be comfortable accepting love. To make the difficult choice to love someone who's difficult to love makes the difficulty of loving yourself less difficult.

This is the relentless wonderworking power of love.

When a car overheats, we don't immediately sell it, trade it or dump it on the side of the road. No, we pull over and look under the hood. We grab some coolant to cool it down. We find water to pour. We have the car towed and worked on until it's in working condition. The same goes for your relationship. Breakups aren't always the solution. You can't keep disposing of things you're too immature, lazy, incompetent or cheap to handle. You have to deal with responsibilities and work through them. But you have to know what's worth fixing.

"Though there were one-hundred reasons to give up, she found one reason to hold on."

We're so complex. If we spent our lives in solitude, we'd be affected by seclusion. If we spent our lives around people, we'd be affected by socialization. In both instances, we'd crave love.

Some people who search for reasons to hold on suffer from issues of confidence.

People aren't born with self-esteem issues. It's a learned behavior that many suffer from. Pay attention to babies. They seek freedom by learning to walk, and gain a sense of independence learning on their own. They don't waste time planning and have the most fun being spontaneous. If they don't get something right, they don't get embarrassed. They immediately try again until it's exactly how they want it. They do things their way. Whether qualified or not, they take risks. They're honest and ask a lot of questions. They're unafraid to express themselves. They value relationships and enjoy life's simple pleasures. They play in life's discoveries and laugh in the face of danger. They believe in the unbelievable and aren't concerned with the real world because imagination takes them wherever they want to go. Imagination is the time travel that lets them see into the future and create their world.

You must ask yourself how we can go from a baby who believes in everything to an adult who believes in nothing? What is society teaching us? What forces are at play to make us believe lies as truth and truth as lies? The more you ask, the more you'll discover.

JANUARY

January // Residue

Their marriage was glitter on feces. They tried to cover it up, and acted like their shit didn't stink. Oh, but it did. Just like yours did once upon a time. Perhaps it still does.

Relationships are beautiful – even the shitty ones. You have the opportunity to grow and experience the world with your best friend. You have access to information you'd never be privy to had you not been with your partner. You can access the experiences that shaped their lives simply by connecting.

They carried heavy baggage. Months after the wedding, they finally decided to unpack.

"Good morning, baby!"

He was still excited by her before noon.

"Hey."

Animosity made her a woman of few words. Never could anything so intimate be so distant.

She began to pull back again. He was oblivious to the subtleties. She was present, but she was still. She was quiet. His love language was acts of service, and she continued doing all the thankless things her husband loved, so he didn't notice when conversations got cut short.

She took the shortcut to loving him, but it was enough for him. She wanted to give more and love fully, but couldn't elude feelings of resentment toward her husband.

He taught her everything she knew – except how to live without him.

She sacrificed her time, energy and efforts on him when it was all a dream. All she got in return was big dick and an empty house. Their home was lovely, but it wasn't warm. They were cordial, but they weren't connecting. She kept it altogether on the exterior, but death was inside of her. Nothing seemed wrong, but not much was right.

If you asked him, everything was perfect. The marriage was just fine from his perspective. He had a ridiculously beautiful wife who he snatched up before she grew up. She'd been down with him for a long while. He built a successful career accompanied with a big home. The only thing missing was an irritating family dog to defecate on hardwood floors.

He went through all of that just to make her smile.

But she wasn't smiling.

She was picking fights just to pick them. Somehow he'd be the one to say sorry. She couldn't even fight him correctly. After a while, he realized being with her was like having a pet chimpanzee – exciting to observe from afar, but at any given moment, she was liable to throw shit at you for no reason.

She hated him for reasons he was unaware of. He didn't understand sexual assault. He didn't know what he'd done is categorized as date rape. She never said a word. She didn't say no. She kissed him back. It was a gray area that hadn't been brought up. He never knew she envied, and even resented his relationship with her deceased mother. She didn't tell him how guilty she felt about the loss of their son. It affected him as much as it did her. They were in too deep from a hole she dug with a shovel of assumptions. It could've been solved with a talk or two. Or three. Having an honest conversation could've made the difference in their marriage. She consumed anger until it consumed her. Residual feelings of abandonment and mistrust never left her. He never said sorry. She never let it go. They went to bed angry.

Morning came and she was afraid of breakfast. It was August's residue serving as a reminder of regret. She should've never entertained her neighbor and his foolish charm. Her smile led to breakfast with the enemy.

Maybe she'd stop smiling.

It led to too many regrets.

She sat sulking in a beautiful vintage chair with hidden cracks at its foundation – just like her. It was less stable than she was; yet she relied on its legs for support in hopes it wouldn't crumble. She leaned on anything that was stronger than her. She hoped marriage would do it, but marriage isn't some establishment greater than the people involved. Marriage is the two people involved. It's only as strong as its weakest link.

"I love you."

He needed to hear it back. He hadn't heard the words in some time.

"I know." She said.

"And I know you need the occasional reminder." He retorted.

They yearned for a love that was right in front of them. When she'd go low, he'd go high so they missed each other. They were two musical notes with a lack of harmony – harsh dissonance. He was the only one straining to get in key.

Oh, I see. You must like a good movie. One that ends well and has all the suspenseful components that force anticipation of arrival like the sensation prior to climax. You were seeking a beautiful storyline. You hoped the grass was greener here to take you away from your own relationship woes. You want a feeling that lasts forever like finally locating an evasive itch on your back with your fingernails.

Scratch that thought.

Green grass grows from bullshit.

SPECIFICATION

"Their marriage was glitter on feces. They tried to cover it up, and acted like their shit didn't stink. Oh, but it did. Just like yours did once upon a time. Perhaps it still does."

The ideal of marriage isn't shit compared to actually being married. Marriage isn't an accomplishment you hang on the wall next to your diploma. Marriage is loving the hell out of someone who is at times unlovable. It's pushing past your level of comfort for the sake of someone else. Marriage is seeing your soul's reflection and chiseling away at every flaw that you've been able to get away with most of your life. It's the blackest, most beautiful, tragic, raw and gorgeous experience ever.

Don't get it twisted!

"She began to pull back again. He was oblivious to the subtleties. She was present, but she was still. She was quiet. His love language was acts of service, and she continued doing all the thankless things her husband loved, so he didn't notice when conversations got cut short.

She took the shortcut to loving him, but it was enough for him. She wanted to give more and love fully, but couldn't elude feelings of resentment toward her husband."

Women who are fed up display their displeasure in different ways. If there's an attitude, there's an issue. Instead of reacting to her attitude, try addressing her actual issue. Find out what it is without allowing your emotions to interfere. If she's being short with you, don't become upset at her for being upset at you. You're fighting fire with fire. Instead, respond in love and genuine concern. If you disagree with her anger and "don't think it's that serious," don't say that. At least show care and concern that she's upset regardless of the reason. That's how you disarm her and get to the issue so you can get out of the gray area and to a solution. You can either keep your pride or keep your woman, but you can't keep both. Pride isn't even tangible. Why do you want it so badly? Where there is pride, destruction is near.

A bad mood doesn't define you, but a bad personality does. Moods are temporary. Personality is defined as the qualities that form a person's distinctive character. It's the energy you consistently give off. Your personality is like a magnetic field that surrounds you and either attracts, or repels whatever it's around. Stop forcing connections with people you don't really like.

Be prepared to release anything God is pulling from you. Claiming dominion over what isn't yours is a game of tug-of-war you're guaranteed to lose. Sometimes not caring can be the greatest kind of care in the world.

If the same reason for the breakup exists after the breakup, it makes no sense to get back together because you miss someone. A pending past resurfaces. Be attentive, track progress and hold each other accountable, or the same tired arguments will reoccur once the sheets dry from the make up sex.

It's unnatural to fight just to stay together. People get a lot of credit for resilience. Resilience is the strength and ability not to break. But what happens to the mentality of such a person? How does trauma affect them?

We must manage the f's we give. If it won't matter in ten minutes, let it go. Gradually build up to it not mattering a day, week, month and year from now. Eventually we won't be giving an f about many of the little things that caused us major stress.

Little fights have large implications.

Whether your significant other is certified crazy or an argument is justifiable, fighting is an obvious sign that something is wrong. It might be something wrong with him. The issue could be with her. It's possible the problem is between both of you. You might not get to an immediate solution, but it's important to note that there is indeed a deeper issue. If it's a relationship issue that occurred during your time together, then a resolution is much more likely to be reached than if the issue is a personal problem your partner had prior to knowing you. This is why it's important to take proper time getting to know a person of interest. Keep in mind that character isn't always revealed in time, but in tough times. Begin as friends and embark in the courting phase as long as it takes to determine who this person is beyond great dates, awesome energy and good vibes. Force over area is the definition of pressure. All relationships experience pressure. If your partner can't handle it, your union won't last. But don't worry – breaking off a romantic connection is less complicated than divorce.

And cheaper.

On to the next one.

I've come to understand that some fights are a part of getting to know each other. They're just a pause in the process. If a fight is based on two people with the same goals – just a different approach, then work through it. Don't run from fights. Get through them and watch your bond grow stronger. When you see a fighter, you're just seeing a spirit that refuses give up.

Sometimes someone's personal journey to self-discovery doesn't include you. You have a dream. Your mind is set. You're focused. God's driving and you're riding shotgun in a two-seater. There's no room for anyone else. Someone calls an Uber to follow you, but you're not slowing up. If someone is serious about showing interest, they'll pump your gas when you pull over. Pray for you on your journey. Contribute to your drive instead of creating roadblocks and detours like it's all about them. If they want to hang around, they must prove there's value in having you near. Be someone that someone else can learn from.

Trust the process. They'll be ready when you are.

"He went through all of that just to make her smile."

All of those things you'd do to get her back if she left you – go ahead and do them now so she doesn't. And don't wait until you have to say nice things to say them. Don't wait until the week after an argument or the moment before bed. Say them now while the tide is low!

You don't work you ass off to get your dream job only to sit back and do nothing once the contract is signed. Relationships require intentional effort that leads to results. Yesterday's wins aren't enough to sustain today's challenges. Don't expect the gifts you got for

Christmas to get you out of today's trouble. You're providing a temporary solution to a perpetual problem. Bandages won't battle bulimia and gratuity can't get you out of a gray area. You're not seeing her or hearing her and that's infuriating her. You're piling up the problems. You probably understand precisely what she needs from you, but it requires you to grow in areas you've been able to avoid your whole life until now. See this as an opportunity for maturation instead of viewing her as a nag. The dope thing about relationships is that they make you better than what made you good prior to knowing each other. That's what they're supposed to do.

FEBRUARY

February // Flu

I t's like a train from London to Paris the way time moves. We begin life full and end life empty. But she was already empty in the beginning.

She was sick and tired of being sick and tired. Breathing was like choking. Whether she fought or surrendered, she suffered from a double-edged sword. She was both the victor and the victim, as any of her wins had unfavorable consequences. Her refusal to give up coupled with her desire to prove herself wrong proved to be a poor pairing. Her marriage was killing her softly. Not the kind of pain strummed with his fingers that Lauryn sang about, but a leisurely extended and torturous death.

They say you have to be born again in order to truly live. So she made a difficult decision. She existed in her current state over what was considered to be the legal limit. It was time to go. So she left.

Not her husband, but her childhood home.

Together, they made the decision to move into a lovely new residence in the hills to call their own. She felt naked and afraid, but free. It was like she finally had permission to begin womanhood. But a harness remained on her hips preventing movement into a newer, better version of herself. She thought the move, multiplied by time, would equal the solution to her sobering issues. But she was still running from home.

When a house is in development, there's an indistinguishable moment where deconstruction and reconstruction appear to be one and the same. Life was that way. All she could see was a mess. She didn't know if she was being built or destroyed — until it hit her like a ton of bricks.

"I'm in love with a memory, not a man."

There, she said it.

Her body was present, but her heart was gone.

She admitted it.

Feeling alone in a marriage felt lonelier than actually being alone. He served a need she no longer had. Something she no longer needed once she realized she had it all along. They both checked out of the union, but their sick determination to win made the days go by.

If you've ever fallen, you know how much it hurts. Falling out of love is just as uncomfortable as falling in love. She hated falling. And she could no longer fall for the lie.

"Marriage, money and good old memories don't mean happiness."

There, she said it.

Now what?

There was a brush of cool air as she got up to walk his way.

"Push!" A loud voice rang. It was her own.

"Breathe!" "You're almost there." She held onto words from the delivery room years ago. They always helped her get through the impossible moments.

She was her own encouragement.

The woman took another step and then went black.

What was said couldn't be remembered, but the look on his face told her she got the point across. As she turned to walk away for the final time, her eyes quickly ballooned with water. She didn't want him to see her crying because she wasn't sad.

Her body finally felt movement.

The air was free.

A woman was born.

"Happy birthday!" A voice like her mother's whispered inside of her.

She exhaled.

In that moment, the woman walking knew she was supposed to be right there. That driveway; their encounter; her hesitance; his distance; the text-back; the great sex; her marriage and now separation; her newfound will to survive all led to this moment. What she thought to be failures were new opportunities. What felt like reduction was growth. There was an immediate shift in the way she decided to approach life.

She picked up a few pounds over the months and she was OK with that. She wasn't worried about taking up too much space. That's a conditional mindset too many women have about their bodies, their homes, their careers and their community. She lost focus on taking up too much space and started saying, "I am enough." It led her on a journey of expanding all the parts of her she was afraid to expand. Not only did she grow, but the universe and others around adjusted to make room for all the love, light, wisdom and beauty her heart had to share.

The next thing to disrupt her happiness was going to have to be rapid, strong and win twice just to beat her once.

And then the cells in her breasts divided.

SPECIFICATION

"She was sick and tired of being sick and tired. Breathing was like choking. Whether she fought or surrendered, she suffered from a double-edged sword. She was both the victor and victim as any of her wins had unfavorable consequences."

Since the beginning of the book, the girl has made a rash of equally good and bad decisions. But sometimes her fate is left in the hands of chance.

Or so it seems.

Often, we search for what's in our hands or wait on prayers that have already been answered. We run in circles backwards like a dyslexic hamster, and blame past people for new disappointments.

We can't see what's in front of us if we keep looking back. Imagine doing that in a car on the highway. It would be crazy to blame other drivers for the wrecks you caused. I'm sure insurance would agree.

There comes a certain point in life where our wounds are self-inflicted. Someone else is responsible for the initial tear, but we keep picking at the scab. We won't let ourselves heal. We blame every bad thing that occurs in life on the people that caused our pain.

Wins are short-lived when you take up space in the past. If it was so bad, why are you still living in a place where there are no tomorrows? There are no sunrises – only sunsets and yesterdays. It's human to be upset; to feel hurt and to experience confusion, but we can't stay there.

If we do, we'll miss sunrise's serenity in the morning.

"Her refusal to give up coupled with her desire to prove herself wrong proved itself to be a poor pairing."

Determination with no direction will get you lost.

Sometimes getting lost leads you down dark pathways into something beautifully unexpected. But most times, you just want to find your way back home.

Every situation the woman finds herself in leads to sadness. She runs from something bad only to crash into something worse. She's out of breath, but she keeps on running.

Many of us have so much to prove to ourselves that we're willing to do anything in order to get to the goal. We practice self-disciplines that aren't consistent with the objective. It's like studying for mathematics before a Spanish test. Ambition, tenacity and endurance are necessary tools to overcome many of life's challenges. However, possessing these qualities without proper direction is dangerous.

A skilled fighter who punches people in a bar gets arrested. A skilled fighter who punches people in a ring gets paid.

It's important to understand that proving yourself wrong must not only be done right, but must also have reasoning. What exactly are you trying to prove and why?

In this case, the woman is trying to prove several things. She wants to show she's nothing like her mother, though deep inside she knows she is. If she took time to understand her mother, she'd see the beauty in that. She's searching to know if she's able to love and receive love. But her process is forceful within a setting intended to be natural. She's a force of nature that destroys what she touches – including herself. Proof proves its power to be destructive when we tamper with its evidence. We don't always need proof to know that something is real.

"If you've ever fallen, you know how much it hurts. Falling out of love is just as uncomfortable as falling in love. She hated falling. And she could no longer fall for the lie."

Honesty makes you uncomfortable because you're cozy when you lie. She was sick of comfort. She needed something to shake up her situation and put her on a path to righteousness. Would you prefer the ugly truth or a pretty lie?

"They say you have to be born again in order to truly live. So she made a decision. She existed in her current state over what was considered to be the legal limit. It was time to go. So she left."

As a new father, I have the daily honor of watching my son experience something for the first time. I get to relive life's easy pleasures and simple joys through his curious brown eyes. I can't recall how it felt to finally stand up on my own two feet, or the moment my tongue touched sugar for the first time. He allows me to slow life down, and for a flicker of a moment, become pure and untainted – uncorrupted by experience.

Human beings are supposed to persist. Being is a noun, but it's also a verb. We are supposed to occur with action, and move about and be. We're in a constant state of motion – whether it is our body, mind or spirit.

All development requires motion. Our survival is dependent on it.

But let's not confuse motion with progress. That hamster on the wheel isn't going anywhere.

The woman wasn't going anywhere either. Her move was just another move to make it appear like she was moving on.

She wasn't.

She was physically in motion often, but mentally in the same place she was as an adolescent in an adult body – like so many others.

At this point in our lives, we must be aware of how we move, who we move, what we move, where we move, when we move and why we move. Our movement should engage our body, mind and spirit. That's why it's important to leave your street, town, city, state and country – and just go. Go somewhere. Anywhere that will encourage growth and development. Connect with strangers and engage your mind.

Challenge yourself to move and track your progress every day. Just make sure you know where you're going.

"In that moment, the woman walking knew she was supposed to be right there. That driveway; their encounter; her hesitance; his distance; the text-back; the great sex; her marriage and now separation; her newfound will to survive all led to this moment. What she thought to be failures were new opportunities. What felt like reduction was growth. There was an immediate shift in the way she decided to approach life."

Life is a series of connected events leading to destiny.

I believe that's what they mean when they say, "Everything in life happens for a reason." Either way, live life with no regrets. Mistakes are just lessons. Make them. But try to make it a one-time thing, not repeat offenses.

"She lost focus on taking up too much space and started saying, "I am enough." It led her on a journey of expanding all the parts of her she was afraid to expand. Not only did she grow, but the universe and others around adjusted to make room for all the love, light, wisdom and beauty her heart had to share."

Life isn't a set of constant rules and guidelines to keep us in line, but gives us room to explore and grow. There's more to living than consumption. We must also be willing to deplete ourselves.

Never be afraid to change. Growth will force us to leave some people we love behind, and that's the most necessary component of it. Love will make you hold on when you know damn well you need to let go. And sometimes to love someone means to let that person go. So go. There will be even more love on the other side. And when the timing is right, those left behind will eventually meet you there. Maybe you just had to arrive first.

You may not yet be who you want to be, but be thankful you're not who you used to be.

The devil is a liar!

When people say you've changed, smile and say thank you.

Have some manners.

The people who swear they know you best don't pronounce your name correctly. The people who know you most think you've changed since they can't reach you directly. It's when you struggle for goals that you're most relatable – but when you reach the goals your relatability becomes debatable. Change leaves a stain some don't like.

It's called growth.

A child is born. If you go away for five years and return, do you expect the child to look, sound, or behave the same? Even as adults, we should be in a state of constant growth. But people expect you to be who you were five years ago. Change is the wrinkled dollar bill one attempts to put in a vending machine – difficult to accept.

Sorry.

Being upset with someone's growth is a sign that you're still in the same sorry place. Bearing witness to bloom should inspire you to mature.

Keep going. Keep growing. Keep changing.

"Marriage, money and good old memories don't mean happiness."

The woman wanted everything her mother didn't have. She figured this was a sure way to never live the lousy life her mom did. She's beginning to see that no matter where she runs, she can't evade her truth.

"And then the cells in her breasts divided."

She's just like her mother. Her realization comes on the day she becomes a woman.

Truth is either cancer that plagues us, or a thing that sets us free.

Happy birthday.

INTERMISSION
052613

Darkness // Light
Whatever light avoids, darkness invades

When white light shines upon black, it appears gray.
The gray area is often a snapshot of travel from darkness toward light
— or light toward darkness.

You decide.

INTERLUDE
SCRIPTURES

Dear Diary...

January 1

 Yo!

It's me. Sorry I haven't written to you in so long. So much is happening!!! I can't believe ~~this shit~~ it happened so fast. Anyway, it's a new year and 1 of my New Year's resolution is to write more so I have someone to talk to. I need a place to put all these thoughts. And. I'm just so...

I cry in the shower so I don't feel the tears.

~~This is stupid.~~

Mother left the home in my name, but ~~to be honest~~ I don't know...it's weird here (here, however you spell it). I don't think we'll stay much longer. We've been looking at new homes in a nice community with breathtaking views. The clouds literally hit you in the face in the backyard. It's the kind of place dreams are made of. I'm ready for something new.

February 22

I can't seem to connect with my husband. He's a decent guy and created a great life for us. He's had his issues in the past, but no one's ever loved me like he does. He's just more interested than I am these days. I feel like I carry the power in the marriage because I don't care about it as much as he does. I wonder if being in love is more torturous than being loved. It's like the worse I treat him, the more he loves me. I think he's trying to convince himself he's a good guy. We've spent more time together this month, but...

~~I don't know. I feel like I should stay married if I want~~

~~to feel a love like this. We've been together forever but~~

~~we're not even friends. He doesn't really know me. He'd~~

~~hate me if he did.~~ It's crazy how you can be around

someone for years and still not know a person...

I got married too young... Too fast. I really wish I would've thought about it or waited. I'm the only one... no married friends or couple-buddies. My girls are single and happy. Taking trips and going all over the world to... like... these...
sexy islands with sexy men. I never got to... I didn't have my moment to ever just have fun. There's still shit I wanna do, you know/ by myself.

....

Or with ~~someone else...~~

Every first I've experienced has been with him. At times I just want my own. Sometimes I feel like I should've smiled and kept walking when he came up to me in high school with his weak game. Haha! But he was so cute. He ~~still is.~~

I go online when I get lonely. I've met up with some of them.

~~I miss my son~~

I had an appointment on Tuesday. I didn't tell anyone. Honestly, it feels good to let this out. Deep down I could tell something was wrong, but I was scared to get it checked out...

I think someone's coming gotta go. Talk soon.

-me ♡

MARCH

March // Pareidolia

She watched old man winter die to spring from her window. Daydreams of better days drifted her eyes to the sky until she started seeing faces in the clouds.

It didn't seem like spring at all. The laughs were few. The sun pushed old man winter out of the way, shining straight through the skylight of her empty home. She was exposed. Her dirt was on display. There was no running from her truth any longer.

Separated,

Orphan,

Cancer patient.

There is no word for a parent who loses a child. That's how awful the loss is.

She poured a second glass of Pinot and looked back to the sky to escape a while longer. The coat of a sheep appeared on a cloud. Soon, its face came into view. She was thinking about herself. She was thinking about her son. She was thinking about childhood and ended innocence. She thought about that which she didn't think about at all. She never allowed herself to. Vulnerability has a way of making us retreat. But she stayed. She allowed herself to feel all the feelings she used to pretend to be numb to. The buildup was incredible. It might've taken a millennium to molder. She didn't cry at her mom's funeral. She only liked her skin wet in one place. She thought about her husband.

It takes a hell of an imagination to see something that isn't there.

He had a clear vision for his family life – a happy wife and healthy son.

Life doesn't work that way.

The best advice I can give is plan to have more plans, then plan for those plans to change.

He planned on calling her, but wanted to give her space.

So he did what all men do when told to never ever call again.

He texted.

"Good morning, Can you chat?"

She wasn't expecting a message – at least not from him.

Then on the third wine pour, she pressed send for the following text message:

"I'd ask for it all back, but you can have it. All my time I gave you is yours. I don't want it back. Anything you gave me is yours. After this text, I'm blocking you. Don't wanna hear you. I'm done. It's over."

She put the wine glass to her lips and threw her head back to splash the remaining liquid into her mouth as quickly as possible. She peered out of the window again.

Silence filled every space in the home.

"Meet me at the gym tomorrow."

She wore a messy bun and bug-eyed aviators with a mirror tint. Tasteful side-boob poured out of a loose fitting cropped tank top. It was faded black. Her yoga pants looked like paint splashed across her thighs, carefully spilled between her legs and slowly dripped down to her calves. They were Capris.

She decided long ago she shouldn't have to put on armor every day she stepped outside. She didn't always want to be at war deciding if her top revealed too much or if her hair down was too desirable. She shouldn't have to avoid eye contact, walk to the other side of the street and speed up to be in crowds to go unnoticed.

So she didn't.

She walked to the front counter where she met a man.

"Thanks for meeting me!" She said with a smile. "Ready to sweat."

"Why would she show up to the gym like this?" He thought.

"Ten kids. We will have ten if you dare adorn yourself in that ensemble again." Salacious words slipped from him.

"What was that?"

"Nah, my cellphone was…doing something."

He followed behind as she strutted to the elliptical machines. All eyes were on her except his. Even some of the women working out were watching.

"Don't look. Do not look!"

He was being respectful, but encouraging thoughts failed. Her body governed every room entered. They were on the final stretch before reaching their destination, when his interested eyes inevitably introduced him to her anatomy. The force of her stride sent ripples up her thighs that made her ass wave like water interrupted.

"I'm gonna use the restroom." It sounded more like a plea than a decision.

She inquisitively turned around and noticed he should've worn briefs instead of boxers. His print and predicament were obvious. It curved to the left as he curved to the left to a family restroom and quickly shut the door behind him. As he collected his thoughts, the door handle slowly started to turn.

"Someone's in here!" His voice pushed out.

The door pushed in.

"I know." A voice said calmly.

She secured her bun, locked the door and grabbed at his pants for what was now hers.

She had options. And she was exercising them.

Push ups and squats.

It was one hell of a workout in the family restroom for the woman with no family.

SPECIFICATION

"She watched old man winter die to spring from her window. Daydreams of better days drifted her eyes to the sky until she started seeing faces in the clouds."

We've all sat back a time or two, tilted our head, and looked at the sky only to see what appeared as the shape of a face in a cloud looking back at us, until slowly drifting and then fading away.

Pareidolia is a psychological phenomenon involving a stimulus wherein the mind perceives a familiar pattern of something where none actually exists. Some of the more common examples are animals, faces, or objects in cloud formations, the man in the moon, and hidden messages within recorded music played in reverse or at higher or lower-than-normal speeds.

Have you experienced this before?

You're not going crazy, are you?

"The sun pushed old man winter out of the way, shining straight through the skylight of her empty home. She was exposed. Her dirt was on display. There was no running from her truth any longer."

This moment of clarity is one the first times we see the woman with a little girl inside of her acknowledge the elephants in her room. We're relieved because we know there's power in isolation. Despite some of her choices, you kind of feel sorry for her. She represents humanity. She's just like many of us. Maybe the woman will finally find solace in solitude.

"The coat of a sheep appeared on a cloud. Soon, its face came into view."

Sheep represent obedience, meekness, patience, innocence and vulnerability. Sheep also represent childhood and self-acceptance. This scene represents the depth of thought the woman was facing and didn't run from.

"She decided long ago she shouldn't have to put on armor every day she stepped outside. She didn't always want to be at war deciding if her top revealed too much or if her hair down was too desirable. She shouldn't have to avoid eye contact, walk to the other side of the street and speed up to be in crowds to go unnoticed.

So she didn't."

She doesn't get dressed with a man on her mind. She isn't soliciting compliments. She's dope because she's dope and she knows she's dope. Her clothing isn't for consumption, but for her comfort. She drapes beautiful coverings over the parts of her she's still working on. Fashion gives her permission to control her narrative. She didn't get dressed to make you feel good. She got dressed to make herself feel great.

Keep walking.

Or feel free to stare if you'd like. She's beautiful, right?

"She secured her bun, locked the door and grabbed at his pants for what was now hers."

There's purpose in everything – even in this book format. No page is wasted. It's intentionally unclear what's happening in this scene, who it is or how it occurred so quickly, but we like it!

"It was one hell of a workout in a family restroom. For the woman with no family."

The woman's pain always seems to resurface or intensify after sex. Take a moment to think about why this is happening.

APRIL

April // Pivot

Life's pivot can be found in the gray. You must travel through dark, murky waters to get there. You will recollect forgotten memories. You have to endure places you swore you'd never revisit. You will face demons head on. You must remove your mask of preternatural calm and lay your fears, terror and distress on the table. You will win if you keep going. You will reap if you do not faint.

"Excuse me."

"Hey!"

"Are you awake?"

The woman opened her eyes to the sight of a stranger hovering over her.

"You scared me – I thought you passed out?"

The man was older than her husband.

He had on dark clothing.

Everything in her said to scream.

She quickly scanned her surroundings and recognized every item in the room. She was at home.

She wasn't sure if she was being robbed or got drunk and let in a Jehovah's Witness.

"Can I kiss you now?"

She'd never been asked for a kiss before.

His coquettish grin was cause for consideration.

"I have somewhere to be. I need you to leave."

The man grabbed his hat and left.

What the fuck was that? The woman was frightened, confused and horny. That's probably the worst, and most dangerous combination when you're alone. She called her estranged husband.

"I need you to come over."

"Now!"

There was a long pause like a page of commas.

"You can't be serious." "I need you to hang up, and go find your mind...you've lost it!"

Dial tone.

The woman couldn't believe it. He'd never spoken to her that way. What the hell was going on?

She called back. No answer.

She dialed again.

She couldn't be alone. She needed somebody immediately.

"You've reached the voicemail of …"

She slammed down the phone causing a small crack on the screen.

She'd been here before, but not like this. She was alone, but not by choice. It felt differently than the times she'd made the decision to leave.

Today was jealous of tomorrow. At least there was possibility there. She was hopeless – undesirable as a cold bath. No one wanted her.

"I have cancer, breast cancer." She texted without explanation.

The doctor confirmed it at an appointment months back.

Tears flushed from her and the phone rang.

"Baby?"

The concern in his voice carried a tone she hadn't heard before. It was like a hug that sent her into another place. The firmest, most thoughtful, warmest embrace received.

"I'm …"

Getting out the words was painful. Every letter hurt.

"Sorry I didn't tell you."

Hearing herself say it made it more real. The cancer was real. He stayed on the phone with her until reaching the front door of their home where he found a woman inside on the floor, beautiful and broken like a fallen chandelier. She didn't look well.

"Baby."

He fell to the floor to embrace his wife where they emptied themselves. They wept through dusk.

Tears filled the foyer.

SPECIFICATION

"Excuse me."

"Hey!"

"Are you awake?"

The woman opened her eyes to the sight of a stranger hovering over her."

The chapter begins as an extension of the prior chapter's last scene. Much like what happens in real life, the woman finds herself caught in a situation she doesn't know how she got in, and is quickly trying to get out of. There are lots of things happening here. The reader is left to read in between the lines and fill in the pages.

"Can I kiss you now?"

She'd never been asked for a kiss before.

His coquettish grin was cause for consideration.

"I have somewhere to be. I need you to leave."

The idea that this woman has the gall to even consider kissing a stranger in her home makes us privy to the complexities of her mental, spiritual and physical state.

Ultimately, she comes to her senses and decides to kick the man out. But for a moment, she considered the idea of doing something completely irresponsible, unsafe and plain crazy – like we all do.

"She called back. No answer.

She dialed again.

She couldn't be alone. She needed somebody immediately."

Emotions are intensified in solitude. There are no distractions. Truth staring you in the face is either an ugly or beautiful thing. Most can't handle when it's ugly so we pile on distractions.

An alcoholic is the same as a workaholic. One ends up lonely in rehab. The other ends up lonely in a large home. Both are escaping something painful.

Pain either encourages withdraw, or stimulates gregariousness. There's no difference from a loner and a social butterfly. On the exterior they're opposites, but internally they both feel more comfortable in a preferred environment.

Our experiences teach us to avoid discomfort. The truth is we should embrace it. Too much comfort kills ambition.

During year three of college, my brother and I were roommates at an apartment in the city. I spent school nights with friends eating pizza, playing X-Box and blasting loud music at our place. There was probably a woman somewhere in my bed waiting on everyone to leave. My brother spent nights coming home late from driving a taxi. At one point, he had a job as a pizza delivery guy. For the life of me, I couldn't understand why or how my brother, who has the same very supportive parents as me, was working as a cab and pizza guy.

What I eventually learned from him will save someone's life. My brother has been wise since I can remember. He stumbled around as an eight year old reading *The Autobiography of Malcolm X* when he should've been getting ready for bedtime. He introduced me to Public Enemy when I was bumping New Kids On The Block.

Back to the story.

My big brother was sagacious enough to cut his safety net and embrace life's challenges to navigate his own way. His choices encouraged personal growth and development. As a result, he matured faster. Meanwhile, I was partying in the suite across from his somber room, accepting an allowance from my parents and comfortably sitting in my safety net with white wine, loafers, legs crossed and no socks on.

Free the ankle.

A few years later my brother was married, in a career and saving for a home.

I was still in school struggling to figure out life.

The illusion of comfort is dangerous. I learned that I'm most comfortable being a bit uncomfortable. It's where I'm most productive and in turn, most effective. I work better under pressure. I waited until the fourth quarter to put a pen to the pages of this book.

We need each other, yes. But sometimes, we need to be alone. It's there that we believe and finally begin to flourish.

"I have cancer … breast cancer."

She texted him with no explanation."

Here lies a simple statement with a profound illustration.

The woman hadn't told anyone about her diagnosis. With all that was weighing on her, it wasn't something she was ready to deal with. The idea that she was so desperate for love, that she was willing to forfeit feelings she protected her whole life, and face truth to receive it, is a demonstration of our deep desire and never-ending need to be loved.

MAY

MAY // MOURNING

H e thought he needed her, until he didn't.
She thought she loved him, until she left him.
What was the reason they remained all this time?

They awoke in a foyer.

Something greater was connecting them. No matter how often they ran apart, they came back together. It was a force beyond natural authority. They were bad for each other, but what was in the both of them was magnetic. Before the sex, they had control. After the sex, they lost control. Something else was in charge now – something more powerful than the both of them.

She often fought against it, but they were fighting to connect.

Days bled. Thursdays weren't her days anymore. She needed to be needed. Her soul was tied. Her chaos needed more chaos. She fed off of him, but her taste was changing.

He was like candy. She was still hungry after him. He whets an appetite, but that's it. She needed a different addiction. She was looking for something to continuously consume after pleasure had been reached. She needed her tongue to be challenged. She wanted someone to devour in excess to the point of illness, but needed him to be her prescription, so she had to taste him in order to survive. She needed to be put to sleep. And tomorrow, repeat.

"May I take your order?"

He had to take a business trip out of state. She agreed it was OK for him to go. She'd been dealing with her diagnosis the last few months without him. What are a few more hours? He promised her he'd be home that evening for dinner.

"Sir, May I take your order?"

"Uh, yes. Sorry."

He was daydreaming of better days at concourse C.

"Easy on the cream, please."

The barista handed the man his coffee and he walked to his gate thinking of his wife at home.

There may be no lonelier place than a busy airport terminal. Kids running around, couples kissing, businessmen with places more important to be – all reminders of what he didn't have.

He knew his wife was mentally checked out of their marriage. While he was searching for her, she was searching for herself.

It's like they never met.

She was here. He was there. She was rare. He knew she was difficult so he studied her. He studied both her actions and reactions. He memorized the curve of her lips – all four. On all fours is what he eventually envisioned her on, but he had to sweep her off her two feet and catch her when she fell for him first. First things first, he must know her name. On second thought, he must find her first. She exists only in his mind, though he thinks she's here.

But she isn't. She's preoccupied celebrating solitude. Independence is trendy, so she dismisses all this is and misses every opportunity to connect. She welcomes the notion of cutting people off and loves to hate so much you'd think she hates love. She does. He wants to meet her, but she doesn't want to be met. She no longer wants be wet, yet she drowns in a pool of her own tears. She loathes being alone, but she loves being independent.

She's better off in his daydreams – no one can get hurt there.

Meanwhile, his wife was at home burying burdens with beer and wine. Drinking was the lubricant that made her truth easier to swallow. She wanted something so badly, but she didn't want him. Her husband was the sweetest, most kind, loving and giving person she knew. He handled her heart like a flower. He not only tended to it when it was beautiful, but he nurtured it when it began to wither. He often sacrificed his own light to resurrect blossom, and in turn, she made him breathe again.

Maybe she didn't want that anymore. Maybe she needed a moment to wallow in the unknown. Her life was full of uncertainty. Perhaps it was time to embrace the haze and enjoy the fog. Maybe she needed to run toward what she was afraid of instead of running from it. That hadn't gotten her anywhere in life thus far.

She wanted to disconnect and exist where everything was a suggestion. Everything was left up to interpretation. Nothing was definite. Nothing was defined. If what she had was the ideal life, she wanted something different.

He disliked gray. Ironically it was her favorite color.

She arrived at the airport to pick up her husband that evening. She was wearing silver – a textured sheath dress with cap sleeves and a gathered upper-bodice. Her back was out.

She pulled up to curbside at arrivals and got out of the car. Pesky law enforcement didn't rush her along – they just watched.

"Evening, ma'am."

"Hey officers."

Her husband glared at the men in uniform and grabbed at his wife's waist to claim possession by embracing her. She grabbed his hands and pushed them away. He settled for a one-armed church hug complete with two pats on the back for good measure. He got a whiff of a familiar scent. It was the smell of her hairspray. It smelled like a woman getting ready.

He wondered why she was decorated in such garments.

"Where are you going? Or should I ask where are you coming from?"

Communication wasn't her thing. She'd rather have Prosecco.

THE GRAY

Silence fell upon her.

She didn't have to answer to his inquiries.

She was living life on her own terms now.

SPECIFICATION

**"He thought he needed her, until he didn't.
She thought she loved him, until she left him.
What was the reason they remained all this time?"**

Don't be like them. Don't stay for the kids. Don't stay to keep up a perception of perfection. If your relationship isn't working, hasn't been working and never worked from the beginning, know when to go. Not many people get it right the first ten times anyway. You're not alone.

There are millions of people who make the mistake of dating a mistake. Some of you are still dating and reading these words wondering what I'll say next. So let me get this correct: you believe that if you've already invested your all into a mistake, you should just keep on investing? I wonder if you feel the same way about drinking bleach after mistaking it for lemon water? Do you keep drinking the bleach after the disgust, nausea and coma, or do you wake up and realize you're in danger, then put measures in place to never make the mistake again?

Poisonous relationships have similar effects. You're disgusted at yourself for staying after all the headaches, but you're stuck in a vegetative state due to time invested and nowhere to go?

Wait.

Would you go to an invisible grocery store, pay an invisible cashier and go home to prepare an invisible dinner paired with invisible red wine? Your relationship is invisible if you're the only one contributing to it. I'm sure your invisible man got you those flowers you bought, huh?

"Maybe she needed a moment to wallow in the unknown. Her life was full of uncertainty. Maybe it was time to embrace the haze and enjoy the fog."

People are afraid to talk about the gray area, but it's where the solutions are. When you finally have those uncomfortable and fearful conversations, you take a relationship to the next level.

As men, most of us just want the problem fixed. We don't want to have long in-depth discussions – we just want to get to the solution, move on and have everything back to normal. But that's the problem. It can't be the way it was until we address the way it is. To clean out a closet you must pile up the mess and organize it accordingly. To clean your closet, you must do the same.

Breaking through is where the trust comes in. You lay yourself and everything else on the table. There's pure vulnerability and trust on the line. It's the greatest place to connect, but no one wants to talk. We'd rather pretend it's all good for photos and friends. We even fool family. But you aren't fooling yourself. You aren't fooling each other. You partner is thinking about the same things you're thinking about. You have the same concerns and questions about the relationship. One of you might be more vocal than the other. One might be better at expressing it. Likely, you're both ignoring the issues.

It's time to talk.

THE GRAY

Today.

Your future depends on it.

And if you decide to breakup, so be it. Maybe it's time for the two of you to finally fly.

"Days bled. Thursdays weren't her days anymore. She needed to be needed. Her soul was tied. Her chaos needed more chaos. She fed off of him, but her taste was changing."

Watch out for that soul tie. Be wise. Be warned.

"He knew his wife was mentally checked out of their marriage. While he was searching for her, she was searching for herself.

It's like they never met."

What they had isn't what they have. Her tomorrows became her yesterdays. Todays don't exist. She resides in history because that's where she knew him. That's where she fell in love. So that's where she remained. There were too many memories; too much planning and predictions with no focus on the moment.

There's right and wrong. There's black and white. But there's also gray. It's the clashing of perspectives. It's hearing all sides of a story. Viewpoints will be different. Memories won't match. People experience things according to their perspective and limitations. And that's not necessarily wrong. People genuinely see the same issue differently based on how they feel. Their emotions influence their experience and their memory. So their stories aren't adding up. It's not that they're lying; it's just that their interpretation of the occurrence is different than yours. The only fix to re-establish the connection is love. Forget the details and just love.

"She wanted to disconnect and exist where everything was a suggestion. Everything was left up to interpretation. Nothing was definite. Nothing was defined. If what she had was the ideal life, she wanted something different."

When man and woman connect, penis connects with vagina, sperm connects with egg, and then connects to uterus and eventually you are born. From birth, your need for connection is rooted in survival. You connect for shelter and food. Unfortunately for some, this trait carries on into adulthood disguised as dinner dates and one-night stands. As you grow, you desire social connection, make friends and maybe something more. Maybe you date, then marry and want a divorce. Even in independence, you seek freedom to connect with what you decide by disconnecting from whatever holds you back.

Sperm's sole purpose in life is to connect to an egg. Communion is natural.

Accept it.

Now let's move on to more important things.

DECEMBER IN JUNE

December In June // Summer Of Sex

We all have a chapter of our lives we don't want read aloud.

She was chasing winter. She saved January drafts and depended on December's dew. They were the months she felt most free. Rose gold sunsets made it feel like summer, but the comforting warmth of whiskey neat reminded her it was December – or was it June? She couldn't care. She lived in her own mind. Her breath was visible indoors, and outside her window was stone gray. Her mind matched the weather. She took a sip of brown hoping to elude the blues. But we all know brown and blue make black. And that's exactly how she felt that feverish forsaken fall – or was it winter?

'Twas cool once the sun fell.

A crisp eve reminded her to grab a coat as she awaited a text back from a guy she'd met online. Somehow she convinced him to cancel a work-related meeting. Maybe this text message helped with negotiations:

"Which one should I wear?"

She sent an image of a single pink thong in luxurious Leavers lace and embroidered tulle laid across a messy bed.

"The other one." He texted back.

He was slick. The alternative was no panties at all.

She liked a man to get straight to the point.

"You feel that?"

"I know you feel it."

"Because I do."

Phony phone foreplay picked up.

She picked up her cell and began to text back, then deleted it. She typed a few more words and deleted them again. There was so much gray in their conversation history – she thought about her husband.

"See you shortly."

They agreed to meet at a coffee shop in the next town over while her husband was at work. She didn't plan on doing much except to sit across the table with no panties on and share casual words over coffee.

She ordered a classic café au lait, waited a few minutes and briefly stepped outside to see if the man she met online was coming. A brisk breeze brushed across her face upon opening the door. It didn't appear he was going to come, so her fingers would ensure she did that evening.

Cold world.

As she pulled out, a car like her husband's pulled in.

The following sunrise, she watched as he rushed to get dressed for a work trip. She made a ritual of this as if trying to convince herself maybe there was still something there. She hated the feeling of feeling nothing when she'd gaze at her beau and he'd suggestively glance back. He noticed the disconnection in her eyes – her pupils dilated whenever she smiled. The deceit on her lips was palpable – he could taste it when she kissed him with open eyes each morning.

"I love you, baby."

Pretending not to know made their marriage last.

She was a slippery one with well-organized schemes. And she knew how to get her way. Once, there was a wealthy guy who asked her on a date she wasn't excited to go on. She turned him down twice knowing arrogance would make him ask a third time. That's when she planned to accept for entertainment purposes only. She left her cheap purse at home and came up with a story that the bag she came with was lost on their date. It was a little white lie that came with a big black bag. As a puppet in her ploy, he offered to replace the purse – a brand new black Chanel purse. She kept the bag and lost his number.

Cold world.

Friday came.

The woman wanted an evening escape. There had been recent commercial development around their home, so she made up a story about checking out a new restaurant in the area.

"You should come." She knew he had to work.

"I have to work."

Alibi accomplished. She was slick like that.

He left and she left.

She was an unintentional narcissist. Her beauty was no opinion at all – it was factual. You couldn't acknowledge her without admitting she was the reason we all have eyes. You didn't have to be skillful with words to suggest her hair was a spilling waterfall.

Imbeciles became poets.

She was a magazine – hair, makeup and fashion. You didn't have to subscribe to anything else because you got it all with her. You could count on her being on trend with subscribers viewing because she was sexy and she knew it – clap your hands.

A round of applause to the woman who had everything and nothing at the same time. You know that fake confidence that comes off as arrogance to protect an overinflated ego as a failed attempt to overcome an obvious fear? Oh, she had all of that and she hid it well. Her insecurities were in her inseams. Her derrière was the distraction. She was well dressed, but wasn't well. Let her walk tell it, her shit didn't stink. But her BS carried a keen odor only his nose could detect.

"Bad lipstick choice."

"Excuse me?" She said.

"Nice shoes, though." He retorted.

"He's gay." She thought.

"It's a Friday. I'm sure your workweek is still going because you look like you don't stop. You appear to have taken delicate time adorning yourself in this adaptable ensemble knowing you wouldn't have ample time to stop by your office, knock out some work, go home to change and arrive on time for your 6:20 dinner date. It's too early for bright lips, love." He disclosed.

"You have ample ass though."

She was appalled!

"Those jeans. Your heels. That blazer paired with that tee…and your skin – all well-dressed." The words effortlessly slipped from him.

"It's only your lips that need undressing."

"Shit!" She thought, and accidentally smiled. It was the most beautiful dis she'd ever heard. She didn't know what to make of this gorgeous slander … this left-handed compliment … this svelte man with a kind of cool that doesn't expire. It was a random encounter, yet he seemed to have known her his entire life. A life she desperately tried to conceal. She had no comeback.

"Thanks." She said coquettishly.

Her script didn't match her smile. She was an easy ready. He knew he had her.

"I'm glad you're on time for our date." He delivered presumptuous words.

"I don't have time to date." She scowled at him with a grimace he wasn't accustomed to getting in good company.

"I'm sorry." He confessed.

She knew she had him.

"You have the same twenty-four hours any anyone else has." He rebutted. "Time is an illusion. We measure it by how often we're able to use it. Some think it's circumstantial, when truly it's a choice. We have time when we choose to make it and whom we choose to make it for." He continued.

"Again, I'm sorry. I thought you were someone else." He was well spoken.

She scowled at him for a second time.

He knew he had her for a third time.

All is fair in tug-of-war.

She ended up on an unplanned date with someone she didn't know.

She preferred dining in. He preferred eating out. She needed a plan, but also enjoyed consensual spontaneity – so he took her in the elevator and planned to pull the emergency stop. They got high on the rooftop. There was nowhere else to go but down. There he ate.

"Wake me if I'm asleep. I demand you tonight..."

She returned home around the same time as her husband.

He forgot to charge her phone. He always plugged it up for her before bed, but this time she didn't want him to. She seduced him sexually to ensure he wouldn't remember. She deliberately made certain her phone battery drained. Earlier that day, she pre-scheduled a phone call with her father-in-law and mentioned to call her husband's phone if she didn't answer hers. Her father-in-law called his son's phone looking for her, and her husband passed her his phone – now she could privately access it without suspicion.

I told you she was slick.

She spoke casually so he suspected nothing while she sifted through his text messages, and he prepped a late night snack for the two of them. She never forgot about the day his car pulled into the coffee shop parking lot at the same time she was leaving. If something was cooking, she was going to find it.

She became upset and surprised when finding nothing of suspicion. In a weird way she wanted her husband to get his, like she was getting hers. He was her cup of tea, but she was drinking champagne now. It was only fair he could sip from another cup. It was the right kind of thinking, right?

He wasn't available to respond to her inner speech. Sleep called him a while ago and he happily answered. She reached for her phone and plugged it up before joining him.

As she adjusted her pillow and curled her legs, her phone lit up.

2:31 a.m. – Scrolling through old messages. She paused on one.

"Hey stranger."

"I demand you tonight …"

Curiosity from the rooftop hadn't left her. If only her husband was awake to tell her to put her phone down and go to sleep. She needed someone to stop her – an older sister or best friend. She knew better, but she was warm. Her bothered blood rushed as decency escaped her. Haunted by what-ifs, she responded to the text.

"Hey bighead…"

The two-word decision responsible for unwanted pregnancies worldwide.

It's gray in the lonely hour.

SPECIFICATION

"She was chasing winter. She saved January drafts and depends on December's dew."

The couple fought a lot in January. She stores the pain in her memory and later uses it as justification to do whatever she wants to do.

Here, the word "drafts" is a double entendre. She holds onto memories of January's weather as a reminder of her freedom. The word "drafts" also refers to the saved email drafts in her email account.

She's conflicted. December is the month she made the decision to intentionally love her husband. She depends on memories of the month's moisture as a reminder of her reason. We all have a purpose for living. He was hers.

"They agreed to meet at a coffee shop in the next town over while her husband was at work. She didn't plan on doing much except to sit across the table with no panties on and share casual words over coffee."

When struggling to break bad habits, we try to convince ourselves we can remain responsible around temptation. It's like a final plea to hold on and prove to ourselves we shall overcome, someday.

One of life's greatest philosophical questions is this: If a woman has no intentions, why'd she show up for coffee with no panties?

Ponder on that. Perhaps there is no answer.

Mostly men have been the ones accused of having ulterior motives in platonic relationships with members of the opposite sex. Our friendships can come into question as if we're holding out for the day a woman is having a weak moment to console her, and then pounce on her like a stray animal.

Gentlemen, be careful.

You'll be most tempted when in committed relationships. You're more desirable when you're unavailable. It's just how this thing works. People want what they can't have. It's the law of supply and demand.

Some women are willing to work around it if you let them. You can give enough energy to be cordial, but becoming too friendly is potentially dangerous. Some women exhibit innocence as a pawn to initiate emotional exchanges that eventually evolve into intimate dialogue. Talks turn to hugs, and hugs are dangerous. Don't be fooled by their squeaky clean image. A hug will have you celebrating Father's Day!

Sometimes just friends are enough. Sometimes you should've kept scrolling past a certain name in your phone. Sometimes you shouldn't have accepted that innocent lunch outing that led to a glance and a smile that should've never happened. Sometimes that Uber should've kept driving. Sometimes you should've stopped at drink number two. Sometimes you shouldn't have let the conversation get so deep, leaving you vulnerable. Sometimes you should've ended the eve early. That long, slow hug goodbye should've never happened. That line should've never been crossed. Those lips should've never touched. That friendship should've never been compromised.

Sometimes.

Sometimes you mistake someone who has been placed in your life for a specific reason as something more than that reason. Don't allow a physical attraction and a weak moment to cause you to reassign someone's position and purpose in your life. Next thing you know, the woman you end up marrying is actually supposed to be the friend who introduces you to your wife.

Dammit.

Be wise.

You've been warned.

"The following sunrise, she watched as he rushed to get dressed for a work trip. She made a ritual of this as if trying to convince herself maybe there was still something there. She hated the feeling of feeling nothing when she'd gaze at her beau and he'd suggestively glance back. He noticed the disconnection in her eyes – her pupils dilated whenever she smiled. The deceit on her lips was palpable – he could taste it when she kissed him with open eyes each morning.

"I love you, baby."

Pretending not to know made their marriage last."

This troubling scene depicts the realized truth of their relationship. They have no business being together, let alone married. It's a relatable scenario for couples everywhere. They find themselves going through the motions, pretending to be in love and forcing sex in front of elephants in the room.

Most relationships fail long before the breakup. We just continue holding onto something that wasn't supposed to be carried by us. The signs are everywhere. The couple in the story even went as far as getting pregnant to guarantee enduring harmony. But glue can't hold a river together.

"Round of applause to the woman who had everything and nothing at the same time. You know that fake confidence that comes off as arrogance to protect an overinflated ego as a failed attempt to overcome an obvious fear? Oh, she hid all of that and hid it well."

Look around, but look closely because you might miss them. These kinds of people are everywhere. Spring warmth brings them out and summer heat causes them surface. They spread their egos across the Internet and smear their insecurities with a brush through hair and across their face.

You know her when you see her.

"Shit!" She thought, and accidentally smiled. It was the most beautiful dis she'd ever heard."

Some women secretly desire men who will put them in their place. This gentleman displays a way to pleasantly accomplish that. However, some women desire even more aggression. Some women don't care for this disrespectful method of connecting altogether. The point is all women aren't some women.

Approach wisely.

"2:31a.m. – Scrolling through old messages. She paused on one.

"Hey stranger."

"I demand you tonight ..."

Be cautious texting at night. Auto-correct will change "pit" to "tit." Don't text your mother after midnight.

INTERLUDE
MUTED

Screaming with the Window Up

A beautiful smile is just a mouth full of teeth.

The only time she smiled was when her body was flung over the end of a bed with her head hanging upside down and a man on top.

But that's not a real smile.

It's an upside down frown.

She danced around an obvious thing. Sex was her favorite form. She did it like a ballerina. The way she exhibited grace amidst discomfort was delightful. She performed the perfect plié on him and made the pain look pleasurable – just like her marriage. She smiled in spite of the sting. She pretended it didn't hurt. She acted as if the stabbing wasn't there. He thought it was enjoyable the way he made her scream. She screamed at him a lot.

She liked it rough.

So she thought.

She adjusted to friction a long time ago. They had a back and forth kind of love, finding balance in the push and pull. He'd push and she'd pull, until pulling too far. Then he'd pull back causing her to come onto him. Whenever he stepped forth, she took a step back so they were always right back where they started.

'Twas a dance that kept her on her toes – and they danced the night away with no lead.

Somewhere in the world, a couple that needs to talk is reserving the right to remain silent.

Arrest them both!

No one can hear you when you're yelling with the window up. It's like talking to yourself in your head and expecting the person next to you to respond. Sounds like the typical relationship, right? Your pleas go unheard and muted thoughts are only opinions in the wind.

Open your mouth.

Your window of opportunity to be heard is short. Soon you'll blow – you'll blow the tires and bust the windows out of the car. Soon is around the corner if you don't open the window to your soul to see when you fail to tell your truth, you're yelling with the window up.

Open your window.

Have a conversation that matters. Ask every question. No one should get upset at questions that involve the nurturing of a relationship. I have a question. Ask yourself why you're in a relationship with someone you can't talk to. Let's start there.

Before you finish, we need to address the elephant in the room.

If you've had the talk time after time, and the message isn't getting through, why are you still standing there? Open the window, climb out and leave. Don't say you're leaving to be cute. Don't threaten to leave to provoke a reaction. Leave because you aren't coming back. Make a decision and stick by it. Either it is or it isn't. When you pull away, you have to commit to pulling away for good or don't pull away at all. At this point, he has no reason to believe you when you say you'll stay away.

Make him believe.

To the Gentleman:

Problems don't always require a therapist, pastor and some Holy oil. They certainly don't require you to grow upset or frustrated.

You'd be surprised at the miraculous breakthroughs a single conversation will accomplish. When you say how you feel, lay it all out and the listener tucks their ego, you can reach an understanding.

Communicate to be understood.

Some people talk to hear themselves. They don't care about the listener other than the available ears provided to unload in. We don't know how to listen to each other. There's always a loaded rebuttal we attack views with. There's no self-censoring. We're not listening to understand – we're listening to reply. We don't want to learn from others, but we demand others hear whatever we have to say. People spew racy rhetoric with no regard to truth. We collect information to affirm ourselves, not to inform ourselves. Communication is a mutual thing. It suggests that a speaker delivered information to a listener who received the delivery, and can appropriately explain and apply the information. They picked up what you put down. Encourage feedback by asking follow-up questions as well as your listener's thoughts throughout the talk. Make it a priority to break things down so they may forever and consistently be broken.

I mean, wouldn't you assume she'd assume if you left her no other choice other than to assume? All that mystery will leave your mysteriously assuming ass by your assuming ass self. Think about what you need to say and say it. It requires honesty about your feelings. It can be uncomfortable, but a woman who loves you won't judge you. She'll treat your thoughts as delicacies and listen with the utmost concern and care to your truth. You'll feel better because of it. So will she.

She was screaming with the window up; a quiet noise that could be felt rumbling from a pit of frustration, forcing her smile to crack inside a mouth full of sin.

JULY

July // Drafts

Summer night's presented sweet orange dusks. They were the kind of sunsets that photographers picked up a camera for. The type that helped mothers explain God to their children. The kind that lovers watched and workers sweated under. Seven o'clock ushered in a cool air. The city came alive.

She didn't. Life was uncertain.

She stopped the dinners and night's out. She was done exploring the wild side she was most curious about. It looked better than it felt. She started looking internally. She used her newfound freedom to express herself fully. She kept a journal that she hardly kept up with, but it was refreshing whenever she wrote in it.

She began writing on her laptop. It gave her a sense of ownership and control over her frantic life. She was able to delete what she despised, cut the future and paste the past to create her own fate. She could write her own storyline complete with everything she'd ever wanted.

She could build a house in the hills with a keyboard. She could tell her husband the things that she didn't have the courage to say to his face. She could be beautiful. She could be young. She could live her life her way.

She could.

SPECIFICATION

"She began writing on her laptop. It gave her a sense of ownership and control over her frantic life. She was able to delete what she despised, cut the future and paste the past to create her own fate. She could write her own storyline complete with everything she'd ever wanted."

We all have a laptop, don't we?

A screen full of selfish selfies below a photo of broke people trying to look wealthy. She wants so badly to be a pin-up so she pins up her hair and puts on short shorts while her short stature poses standing carefully atop of unread novels, hoping they don't topple – followed by the hashtag #LifeOfAWorkingModel. Though it's intended to look like a coincidence, his camera phone is perfectly positioned to capture the luxury car emblem on the steering wheel of his father's vehicle – the caption reads, "What ballers do." Rent is past due, but you can't tell by uninterrupted posts of all his shoes. Sadly, his social network represents all of him. I hope his landlord doesn't follow him.

You just don't understand…they do it for the 'Gram!

Social media is a cool and quirky way to stay connected through photos. It's great for two things: sharing moments of your life, brand or business or the life, brand or businesses of someone else. Most people front and do the latter. Either that, or their life is a reality show that they don't get paid for. They have no known notable achievements, but they want to be known. They couldn't get a reality TV contract, so they settled for a username and password.

Picture this: a beautiful lady walking down Madison and Fifth Avenue in New York City. Her phone camera obstructs her view as she shamelessly snaps selfies in front of flagship stores. Her caption says, "Shopping," although she holds no bags.

She can't wait to get to the club, only to get to the club, talk to no one, dance with no one and take shots the entire evening as if enjoying herself. Not drink, but selfies. You should see the expression on her face once she puts her phone down.

Her photo says "No filter" while the world is thinking, "No thank you." Super model shots in dresses with the hashtag #Bored. Yes, we see the ironing board in the bathroom with your dirty toilet seat up.

Her profile says actress: 150k followers, but she sleeps on an air mattress. They're famous for nothing. Will someone please say something?

I didn't write this to judge you. You'll do that on your own time.

Live more. Post less.

ONSET OF AUGUST

Onset Of August //Atonement

Dinnertime was at one in the afternoon so she could rush to bed. She didn't want to be up. Being awake was a reminder of reality. Having a nightmare couldn't be worse than living one.

From her breasts to her brain.

That's how he used to love her. He'd examined her existence by every inch and depth.

From her breasts to her brain.

That's where her bosom housed a hardened heart. She never made the connection between the two organs. Her heart depended on love to survive. Her mind clogged her arteries.

From the breasts to the brain.

That's where her cancer spread. She was mixing medicines, months and days. Mixing imagination with reality. Confusion was a constant state of being for the woman with dark hair.

She was tired.

She had chemotherapy after surgery. Her CAT scan showed she had massive brain lesions. She had a craniology, then radiation therapy along with more chemotherapy.

She was tired of all the questions.

They told her the cancer was gone, and then it showed up in her brain.

"Am I going to die?" "How long do I have to live?" "They said 98% of breast cancer patients survive – is it the same for brain cancer?"

High and lows.

It's like a life being saved and murdered in the same sentence. It's the leftover pie-box with no pie left in it. It's getting married and then divorced. It's the same as birthing a stillborn baby – joy and pain.

Distraught.

She's been at war her entire life. Just when she sees a win, she's losing with five seconds left in the game. And she scores at the buzzer. And the referee says your points don't count. She always perseveres and beats all odds. They say it's a miracle right before they say, "I'm sorry, your cancer is back."

Broken.

Mind. Body. Spirit.

The clock appears to be on the same hour every day. Mornings feel like evenings. Sometimes it gets really dark. It's usually dark. He feels like he's losing her. She feels like she's lost.

He looks at her laptop. There are drafts dated January and December. What he found upon scrolling further broke his heart. Stories. Emails. There were outlines of unaddressed and unsent messages of affairs and other intimacies that sounded like moments shared with him.

His moments.

The End.

SPECIFICATION

"From her breasts to her brain."

When it's unbearable, you speed through it.

"The clock appears to be on the same hour every day. Mornings feel like evenings."

When it's unbearable, you speed through it.

"The End."

When it's unbearable, you speed through it.

REVELATION

Revelation // Way, Truth, Life

A ll things beautiful were at her disposal. She reached for what was most beautiful. She reached her hand to glory. Then disconnected.

She saw hope when she suffocated.

She let go.

Breathe.

At that moment, she realized she had a profound connection to everything. A vast power is ever at work, giving us the illusion that we are not moving when we—and all things—are actually in constant motion. And so the bride and groom in that still moment by the bed in the hospital room feel the God whose love creates energizes and preserves, and calls those made in his image to participate in his divine humility by losing their life in order to gain it.

Death is the evidence that one's mission is complete.

And then she let it all go. The good and the bad – it did not matter. Pain no longer held her down. Love carried her through.

You can breathe now.

She was not the best wife. But she was his wife.

And she was home.

And she was gone.

Devastation.

He could not breathe.

The air was not there.

His world caved in.

Why??

Why????

No, no no!

There was a lot of shoe leather – they traveled a long dusty road.

He drifted early that day at the rose pink light of dawn. With eyes wide shut, he saw his wife and son off in the distance. In his father's hands was a small book with ruled pages bearing the son's name.

Read the fine print: Much of the gray area is confusing. Usually, what is intended to confuse you is intended to harm you.

Getting out of the gray often involves doing things that appear counterproductive to our beliefs. Love those who hate. Forgive those who hurt. Run toward pain, and not away from it. Embrace struggle and avoid comfort. Question society. Believe in the unseen.

Love is found outside of darkness and toward light. It gets gray in the middle and that is OK as long as you keep journeying toward light. Do not turn around. Do not go back. You will be tempted by past pleasures and previous people still stuck there. But you know exactly what is waiting for you in the past. You have been there before.

Basic human desire consists of acceptance, approval and belonging with the ultimate desire of connecting. Connection is physically illustrated in everyday relationships. We desire to get closer, and closer. It is a never ending journey until we reach The Source.

Take a look around. There is relationship within all things. We have a universal connection to everything around us and beyond. To fight this is to fight the very reason we breathe. We are suffocating. We are fighting for air and space that is infinite, and killing to survive an inevitable death of a life we know little about.

We should know a few things. The first is we are not in control. Do not be fooled by presidencies and rulers. Do not place faith or fate in woman or man. We are either governed by love, or we are controlled by sin. There is no in-between.

Do not be shaken by fear and divisiveness, but be moved to love. Do not be distracted by falsehood and death, but be moved to love. Do not condemn your counterpart and worship your competitor. Be moved to love.

Hope is the light that cuts through the gray.

Balance is the ship that keeps us afloat in gray.

Love is the weapon that destroys the gray.

Love is the greatest connector. It consumes what it contacts. Negativity surrenders to its power. It converts negative energy to positive. Love is patient. It is kind. Love does not envy or boast, is not proud, does not dishonor, is not self-seeking, easily angered, keeps no record of wrongs, does not delight in evil but rejoices in truth and always protects, trusts, hopes and preserves. Ever tried hating someone who insists on loving you? It is almost impossible. We all give in to love's overwhelming force. It has the power to conquer all. The more we love, the more we are available to receive love. It is contagious. You have to give more in order to see more. If we fail to see love, we fail to see ourselves. We are made from love by The One Who is love. The more you hate, the more you receive hate. It is how this thing works. Love is the only way in.

The way we treat each other is a reflection of the way we see each other. The way we see each other is a reflection of how we see ourselves. How we see ourselves is a reflection of how we see our Creator.

Because a blind man cannot see the sunset, does the sun not exist?

You would not have made it this far in the book if you were not searching for more.

Opinions—even good ones—are interesting, but too many—including mine—can cloud your thoughts making matters worse. Instead, reach internally to The still Voice that dwells deep. The Voice that knows you better than you know yourself. That is The Voice that will direct your path away from the gray.

Stay in motion. Let us journey together. I commit to running, walking and stopping with you. We all should be wishing people well. We need it. There is strength in numbers. With all the division in this country, they are beating us. But it is written that we will win.

If you stare at your neighbor long enough, you begin to see yourself.

On a road full of cars, a bus full of passengers, in a room full of strangers and a man on a park bench – someone has suffered something horrific. Something terrifying. People we see everyday have quietly suffered something so disgustingly traumatic that we would never know about. People are walking around with battle wounds and the belief that there is no way out. There is no escape from the dark cloud that consumes them.

People are people. Some are fickle, and others have thick skin. You never know what you are going to get when meeting someone new. You might get along with a neighbor one day and then they give you the cold shoulder the next. It could have been something as simple as a missed invite to watch the game, and your neighbor never speaks to you again. When you disrupt a connection, there is friction. It creates turmoil. If you text while dating or ignore someone, you interfere with the flow. You are considered rude. But when you respect someone enough to listen, look and give that person your full attention, the connection continues allowing a continuous flow of clean energy called love. It is an everyday example that we are created to connect.

Life is about relationships.

Kindness should not be a gift given to the deserving. It should be available to everyone and given generously. Because if you do not give the world your kindness, what is the alternative? What are you giving?

Humanity is such a beautiful concept. Let us make it work.

We all want relationships. Whether it is with someone or something, we have an innate desire to connect. Just like a child needs a connection to parents, The Creator created us in His image, and we desire a connection with Him. Some mistake money as the source. Some mistake power, or sex as the source. But the Source is the Creator of all of these things. You do not connect to a byproduct; you connect to its creator.

I am more fascinated by the artist than the art.

There is no such thing as happenstance. Coincidence is a word for people who cannot explain God. You read these words on purpose.

Always explore that purpose.

SPECIFICATION

Present day…

ESTELLE

Epilogue: By Estelle

Very seldom do the words come along that explain the gray area of your overall life.

I've personally been in the pages of this book as long as I've known myself as a teenager and as an adult and whatever it is that I am now. More specifically I've always found myself in the gray post-breakup. I've been the one "losing weight, looking great, changing my hair, being forced to take inventory, deciding if I want to fix it, move on or exist through it – offering what I've learned while not taking responsibility for anything or anyone but myself." And to my credit, I think I'm getting better with each breakup and just trying to figure out life…

Indeed, I believe it shows up in the music and songs I choose to sing.

Recently I've started to take inventory and just be better at getting better – Yes folks, I know this sounds like millennial talk – stay with me:

o *I've been paying attention to how to be better in relationships without breaking up with someone. General psychology says that you tend to react to life experiences based on your past. My Dad left when I was 3 and returned when I was 23 so you know, rejection issues – much like everybody else.*

o *I've been paying attention to how to make sure I don't repeat the crappy actions of my ancestors and then elders in my today world. Elders, I'm sure some at the time were doing best they could making the best decisions given their circumstances. I'm sure.*

○ *I've been paying attention to what I want my legacy to be – not just workwise, but in life everyday and the future.*
This book is a touchstone, a space to ensure you're not going off into the wild while continuing to build your better, faster, stronger town – aka you.

And I hope your town is filled with color...

-Estelle

Grammy award-winning singer, songwriter, record producer, actress, incredible human and CEO

ADIEU

ACKNOWLEDGEMENTS

This is the book that didn't want to be written. It's the most difficult thing I've done. I finished it the day before it released to the public. That's how much I wanted to say. That's how much I want you to heal…me to heal…us to heal.

Nothing but the power of Jesus. God got me through this. If you only knew. Christ isn't some mythical creature. He is my all and all. I submit all to you, Father. I am nothing without you. I couldn't be; I couldn't breathe. I worship you entirely. I thank you, Lord. Thank You. Thank You. Thank You. I don't believe in You because my parents made me do it, or because I'm a gullible fool – I believe in You because You revealed Yourself to me a long time ago. Our relationship is personal. You saved me. You save me. You're saving me. You've never left me or hurt me. I don't always understand, but I'm not qualified to. If I understood, I still wouldn't understand. I'm not created to understand You. I'm made to love You. I'm made to love Your creation. I don't need to understand. I just want to honor You. My soul is forever desperate for you. Forgive me where I fall short. I just love you, and I thank You.

He is real!

Dear Heavenly Father, I pray that souls are healed. I pray bodies are made whole, again. I pray a nation and a world is delivered from darkness disguised as daylight. Open our eyes so that we may see Your glory and recognize that it comes from You. I pray away strongholds and generational curses.

Freedom!

Freedom!!

Freedom!!!

It is finished. This is it! God is good. Thank you, Lord. Thank you for your faithfulness and your favor. I pray this book is used for your glory. Let it reach millions. Let these words touch lives and move through communities. Let it shift culture and impact generations. Let it tremble the world. The praise is Yours. All criticism is mine. More of you, Lord...less of me. If there is anyone reading these words that might be going through something they feel they can't get through alone, show them Your glory. Bless every reader of this book. Shift their spirit. Open the floodgates of heaven and show them Your love.

TO WHOM IT MAY CONCERN: It will all work out in your favor–in Jesus name. Keep pushing. Keep going. Don't stop no matter the size of the mountain.
Amen.
To my wife.

You.

Period, no ellipses.

Your name alone is a strong enough sentence; a powerful enough paragraph; a big beautiful book. You are all things. I owe it all to you. You are my reason. I apologize for taking so much time in solitude to work on something I'm childish to believe will change the world. You believe in all my silly ideas because you believe in me. I believe in myself because of you. We work best together. I'm a better man because you breathe. I'm a proud father because you're a living piece of art I had to touch...have to touch! There's God, and then there's you.

And then there's Miles! My son, you don't yet understand that daddy's a dreamer who writes to try to save the world, you just know that daddy's not always home for playtime. Just know that you are with me everywhere I go. You're a part of all of my thoughts and decisions. But none of that adult-talk matters. You just want daddy to pick you up and fold you over his arms so you can fly. Daddy wants you to fly too, son. Seeing you soar is the reason I'm not always home for playtime. However, now that this book is finished, daddy will be there every night you go to sleep and each morning you wake so I can pick you up, fold you over my arms and let you fly!

To the minds and memories I invaded to craft this story, I hope gave it justice. I hope you are healed. I hope you move on.

To the supporters and readers, you're the reason I write. I have a shoe-on-the-other-foot style that sets out to broaden your perspective. My words are written for understanding. My goal is for each of you to be more understanding and less judgmental while telling you the truth. Thank you for listening and rocking with me for all this time. I don't consider you fans–I consider you fam.

Charlina Allen Pruitt is the sweetest, most humble and efficient editor I know! Thank you so much for the long nights and frequent emails. Thank you to Latoya Smith of LCS Literary Services for formatting.
To the other dope women in my life (alive and away)! Grandma Frettie Jackson, Arlene Amaker, Gwynne Toney (Mommy), Auntie Jacque, Auntie Bolaji, Auntie Bose, Auntie Brenda, Aunt Celeste, Mrs. Gail Bereola, Nikke Bereola, Abigail Bereola, Angela Bereola, Queen Adanya Bereola, Sheri Lawson, Lisa Bush, Coreen Carroll, Cousins Cassandra and Vivian Jackson, DaNeisha Goode, Jordyn Goode, Brooklyn Jackson, Adjele Frank, Therese and Georgia Onyemem, The Swann Ladies.

I didn't do this alone. Thank you grandpa Luther Jackson (*Psalms 27*), and my daddy, Rev. Olu Bereola. I'll never be too grown to refer to you as, daddy! Thank you Pops aka Bruce Toney. Thank you to the genius that is my Creative Director, Justin Huff. We're the Snoop and Dre of books and book covers! Let's work on a film next! Thank you to Ajay Relan for posting the photo on Facebook that sparked an idea in my head and inspired this book cover. Thanks to my manager Jerrund Wilkerson II. Christopher Gray Parsons you killed the photography inserts. Blessed to have you a part of 2 books in the series. Get better Uncle Earl Nichols. Pure love to Pastor J. Alfred Smith Jr. and the Allen Temple Baptist Church family, South Bay Community Church family, Kenny Burns, Rahman Grayson, Chloe Williams, Nadeen Gayle, The Carroll Family, Jacque Diamond, Skyler Grey, Holman Arthurs, Tony Gaskins Jr., Rob Hill Sr., Dr. Alex Ellis, Remi Bereola for being big bro, Ryan Bush for being family and assisting in digital marketing, Gary Banks II for being a beacon of light and encouragement at all times for over 20 years! Thanks to Dr. Idoroenyi Amanam for answering all medical-related questions in the book, Jonathan Bullock for constant support and excitement for this one, James Freddie Johnson III for always being there no matter what, Everett Frampton for lifetime loyalty, Johnathan McGriff for calling to make sure I was doing OK writing this, Johnnie Tangle III, Tommy Fulcher, Zeke Ivy, Matthew Heisser, Robert Douglas, Kenneth Whalum III, Kings of Leon, Elujay (dopest artist in Oakland, CA), Radiohead, Emeli Sandé, D'Angelo, Common, Sinatra, Jon Saxx, DJ Mike Tee, Miguel, J.Cole and John Mayer for making inspiration to write to. Thank you Malcolm Marshall, *Street Soldiers* Radio, Uncle Dwight, JQ, Hunter Jackson, Nbueke and Jit Lassey, Charles Onyemem, Prince Kaden Justice Bereola and Daijon Bereola – I'm so proud of you. Thank you to "Classic Man" Jidenna for the model manifesto and Estelle for the epic epilogue. The two of you are on a mission to heal the world. Thank you for lending your words to something real.

Thank you to all those who contributed portions to the book: You're changing lives! Thanks to the barbershops and hair salons that will speak of this book for years to come. Thank you to everyone spreading the word. Keep talking!

If I forgot anyone, I've got a son now...I forget everything! Perhaps I'll take you for wine while at work one of these Wednesdays. That means never.

Cheers to the people and partnerships who don't support me at all. You're free fuel for my fire. And fuel is expensive, so thanks again!

Pour some champagne.

"Blessed are you when people insult you, persecute you and falsely say all kinds of evil against you because of Me." –**Matthew 5:11**

ABOUT THE AUTHOR
Enitan O. Bereola, II

Has taken the stale concept of etiquette and made it tasteful, again! He penned the award-winning and best-selling books, *BEREOLAESQUE: The Contemporary Gentleman & Etiquette book for the Urban Sophisticate* and *GENTLEWOMAN: Etiquette for a Lady, from a Gentleman.* His third title, *THE GRAY: A Relationship Etiquette Study* debuted as fine art at the world's premier international art fair – Art Basel in Miami Beach, FL.

Enitan is Chief Executive Officer of The Bereolaesque Group. As a cultural figure, he's a powerful speaker, producer and sought after celebrity ghostwriter whose voice reaches generations. He consulted and partnered with 20th Century Fox, Apple, Facebook, Salesforce, Visa, Elastic, Accenture, LINKEDIN, Yahoo, McKesson, Brown-Forman, Crown Royal XO, Jack Daniels, I.W. Harper, Anheuser-Busch, BEVEL, Bergdorf Goodman and Goorin Bros. Bereola worked on projects with Award-winning Actors Hill Harper & Meagan Good, Congresswoman Barbara Lee, Michelle Williams of Destiny's Child, Grammy Award-Winning Platinum Producer Bryan-Michael Cox and others. President Barack Obama & the First Family, Oprah Winfrey and Mark Zuckerberg are owners of his work.

The Bereolaesque brand garners interests of dignitaries, celebrities and pop-culture alike. He paired up with Beats By Dre's "Show Your Color" campaign to spread his gentleman message, as well as Jay-Z and Steve Stoute's Translation, LLC advertising & marketing company. Bereola produced an international soundtrack to his first book entitled, "Seat 1-A," and the short film, "This Time," which debuted at film festivals around the country.
Enitan Bereola II is the recipient of the 30 Under 30™Award Presented by Porsche, Equanimity's: Best Story Told Award, BC award for Greatness in Literature, Shades Wedding Magazine "Man of the Year"

award and other decorated honors. Bereola's been selected as one of BLACK ENTERPRISE Magazine's Young and Bold Business Leaders. He's exercised etiquette on FOX News, dished dating advice to NBC Niteside, talked tips on TV One with Roland Martin, and debriefed with BET and MTV. He's a regular on California's 106.1 KMEL "Street Soldiers" and his writings have been discussed on nationally syndicated radio. Bereola's been featured on the covers of Equanimity, American Dreaming, Ambition and Shades Wedding magazine, as well as the cover of Detroit's Front Page Paper. He's also featured in Essence, Upscale, Juicy, Sister 2 Sister, Los Angeles Sentinel, Naija Times in Nigeria and other notable publications.

Enitan partnered with the Alice E. Foster Scholarship Program through the San Jose Links, Inc., who sponsors scholarships for high school graduates exiting the foster care system. The author ran a program to adopt his former high school – Piedmont Hills, to contribute 20% of his Barnes & Noble book sales to help fund student programs. He also partnered with Autism Speaks through American Dreaming Magazine, who donates 100% of profits from POP displays at retailers. He supports The Bay Area After-School All-Stars and joined forces with the Crohn's and Colitis Foundation of America to help their mission to fund research and programs.

Bereola has been a keynote speaker at over 50 colleges and universities. He's been invited to speak at Harvard, Stanford and Tufts. The first book is a required part of Bermuda College and Kansas State University's curriculum. The second book is a translated top-seller in Lithuania.

Bereola attended Florida A&M University. He is on a world tour.

Contact: info@Graynovel.com

Let's make a film of this…

PLAN A

<u>PLAN B</u>

IV

52464217R00150

Made in the USA
Columbia, SC
03 March 2019